A Guide to Canoeing the Missouri River

A Guide to
Canoeing the Missouri River

by Keith Drury *"Second Wind"*
Available from:
Indiana Wesleyan University Bookstore
4201 South Washington Street
Marion, Indiana 46953
765-677-2210

> Presented to future canoe trekkers as a public service of the Camping and Retreats class of Indiana Wesleyan University.
>
> Indiana Wesleyan University
> 4201 South Washington Street
> Marion, Indiana 46953

Online edition and updates:
http://www.indwes.edu/courses/kd-ced454/guide.html

Premiere Publishing
Indianapolis, Indiana

First Edition   July 1999
1999, All rights reserved, Keith Drury
ISBN 0-9664049-3-9

While the information in this guide may not be reproduced for sale without the written approval of the author, you are welcome to make copies for actual canoe trekking adventures

A trek...
a journey...
a pilgrimage...

Dedicated to those who
understand the reasons why.

Contents

Chapter 1. SO YOU WANT TO CANOE THE MISSOURI RIVER?
Here's what you've got in store...Page 8

Chapter 2. GEAR
A helpful list of gear   Page 19

Chapter 3. TIPS AND HINTS
Ideas, tips, and hints   Page 30

Chapter 4. My Day-By-Day DIARY:
One man's trek down the river   Page 40

Chapter 5. TREKKING DATA
A point-by-point guide   Page 88

Chapter 6. AFTER YOUR TREK
Words to the recently finished   Page 127

Chapter 7: Tribute to a River
The route becomes a companion Page 130

Chapter 8: A Short Book List
To read before and during   Page 135

Introduction

I never intended to write this guide. The notion of canoeing the entire Missouri River occurred to me as a teen, but I had filed it in the back of my mind under "Dreams-I'll-probably-never-realize." That is, until I read Steven Ambrose's *Undaunted Courage* and decided the time was right.

In making preparations for my journey (as a backpacker undertaking a canoe trek) I had a hundred questions: Where to get groceries? How do I get around the dams? Can I camp anywhere or are there restrictions? Who are the contact people and what maps can I use? As an Appalachian Trail hiker I assumed there would be a "Data Book" or "Wingfoot Guide" for the Missouri.

But I found none. There were bits and pieces of information, but none designed specifically for the canoe or kayak. I determined to write one.

So, I had to take my trek "blind," stopping in all of the wrong places to discover where I should have stopped, over-packing supplies because I did not know of re-supply points ahead, and finding out who would have helped me if I had known, only a day later.

This guide was written on-river tapped into a tiny palm-top computer each night before I went to sleep from my notebook scrawling through the day. I hope future trekkers will correct, and augment this guide. It is available free on the Internet and in a handy pocket size edition for easy carrying on your trek. Updates will be issued regularly and you are welcomed to submit them to the author at: kdrury@indwes.edu

Keith Drury
Marion, Indiana July 1999
4201 South Washington Street
Marion, Indiana 46953

1

So You Want to Canoe the Missouri River?

Here's what you've got in store...

THREE FORKS, MONTANA
You are in for the trek of your life! Putting in a narrow swift-running rock-bottomed clear stream at Three Forks, Montana you'll keep looking back over your shoulder at the snow-capped Bitterroot Mountains where Lewis and Clark crossed to the Columbia River. Soon you'll be portaging around your first dam, Toston dam, a tiny one, but an indicator of what's ahead in the first two thirds of your journey: 14 dams to portage before you get totally free waters in the final 700 miles to St. Louis.

CANYON FERRY LAKE
At Townsend you'll enter your first big lake, Canyon Ferry Lake, infamous for its abrupt storms where the rollers can get higher than your boat is long. You'll keep your eye on the sky while on this beautiful lake. It can also be a smooth as glass, especially if you canoe it in the late evening as the sun is setting.

GATES OF THE MOUNTAINS
After a horrendous portage around Canyon Ferry dam you'll pop around two smaller dams,

Hauser and Holter, then roar down Wolf Creek Canyon where you'll swear the river looks like a gradual descending hill for several dozen miles. Steep canyon walls tower above you before the river slows and begins to meander toward Great Falls. Watch for sheep on those cliffs.

GREAT FALLS
It took Lewis and Clark a month to portage around this series of falls, dropping four times more feet than Niagara. There are five dams here, but if you know how to connect with the local canoe club, it won't take you a month, but only a day (see data chapter for phone number of contact). While in Great Falls you'll probably visit the Lewis & Clark Interpretive center, world famous for its excellence. Maybe you'll see the largest spring in the world nearby as well. Discovered by Lewis and Clark, it boils out of the ground at river-rate. (It is also considered the "shortest river in the world") Below the Great Falls you'll just have a short hop to Ft. Benton, the "upper end of the line" during the steamboat era. In the late 1800's Ft. Benton was Denver. If you didn't plan a motel night for this delightful tiny historic town, you'll wish you had.

WILD AND SCENIC RIVER
Just out of Ft. Benton you'll enter the National Wild and Scenic River section, which, combined with the following section, is the most remote run on the river. Towering cliffs rise from the river's edge where you'll see mountain sheep skipping about on rock-climbing cliffs. You'll get out and climb up into the "Hole in the Wall" a three-people size hole

right through a sandstone wall perched high above the river. You'll use one of those panoramic disposable cameras to snap awe-inspiring photos thorough the hole. Continuing on you'll meet Grace Sanford, in her 80's yet stills running the dirt-road (not gravel, but a real dirt-road) ferry several times a day in this remote land. "Oh, sometimes we get real busy on weekends and I run it over ten times." Trees are so rare in this section they are marked on the maps. And they are in demand for campsites to escape the blazing heat of the Big Sky sun.

FORT PECK LAKE

But your wilderness is not finished yet. Immediately upon leaving the Wild and Scenic River you'll enter two adjacent wildlife refuges surrounding the 130 mile long Ft. Peck Lake. And what a lake it is! Remote, large, and packed with wildlife you'll love this wild and scenic lake. So far on your trek you'll have already seen mountain sheep, elk, pronghorn antelopes, mule deer galore, white tailed deer, prairie dogs (Lewis & Clark called them "Barking squirrels," probably a better name) the tiny swift fox, maybe a badger, a black-footed ferret, and a long tailed weasel, plenty of beavers and whole beaver-cut forests, maybe a coyote or two, (at least you heard them) plus a myriad of birds including the constantly cheerful Western Meadowlark, the white Snowy Owl, the Sharp-tailed Grouse, Sand hill crane, Upland Sandpiper, Golden and Bald Eagles, and thousands of White Pelicans plus scores of species of ducks. The whole trek so far has been one elongated wildlife refuge, and you are just now entering the official ones!

You'll probably be storm bound a day or two on Ft. Peck Lake, but you won't care -- you'll take plenty of extra food and you'll snuggle up in your cozy tent and catch up on your reading in the Lewis & Clark journals or write letters home. You'll end up your 300 miles of wilderness by staying at the Ft. Peck Hotel, the original building constructed when 30,000 people rushed to find jobs during the depression in this grand WPA-FDR type project. Other than a 60's style carpet upgrade everything, else is pretty much unchanged since the Depression. You'll love your stay and the hotel management will go out of their way to make trekkers like you feel welcome, right down to fetching you and your boat from the landing, saving you the mile long portage.

TO THE CONFLUENCE

Below Ft. Peck Dam the river is usually shallow and meandering, and you'll coast down the lazy curves now with whole forests of cottonwood trees and willow bottoms lining the banks. Here you may discover several places where you can still ford the river without getting over your head. The river here is bordered by Indian Reservations.

Then you'll stop at Ft. Union, a completely reconstructed trading fort before canoeing the short hop to the confluence of the Missouri and Yellowstone. The red-mud Yellowstone, if you hit this spot in early June, will be swollen with snow melt from Yellowstone Park and the Rocky Mountains. (Sorry, the Yellowstone is not yellow but red. Yellow is reserved for the Osage, much later down stream.) This new surge of water volume will speed you along into the next lake.

LAKE SAKAKAWEA

As you pass Williston you'll wonder if you'll ever escape the tangled spaghetti bowl channels, backwaters, and oxbows of the Williston Marsh. But you'll keep following the current and eventually you'll come out on the delightfully beautiful Sakakawea Lake, named for the Indian woman guide and interpreter who accompanied Lewis and Clark (with her little boy on her back!) Dakotans spell and pronounce her name differently than the official USA mint pronunciation, and they insist they are correct. If you say otherwise they'll enjoy an argument with you. And they'll enjoy winning.

Lake Sakakawea is usually called "the river" by those who live near it, running some 175 miles, narrow and long, bordered by lush green hillsides and herds of range cattle. Perhaps it will be on this lake where you sleep tentless and see what the Big Sky looks like at night. Maybe you'll have purchased one of those glow-in-the dark sky maps and here is where you'll learn a dozen new constellations. Also, the endangered Whooping Crane uses this lake as a rest stop in its migrations. After many days you'll arrive at Garrison Dam, signaling the end of this delightful long and narrow lake. There is yet another long narrow lake-river ahead of you. But you must stop in Bismarck first.

GARRISON DAM TO BISMARCK ND

You'll be both happy and irritated to be back on the river. Happy to have a current again, but irritated at the sand bars and snags. You'll most likely stop at the excellent Lewis and Clark Center in Washburn ND and see a hand-made 30' cottonwood dugout canoe fashioned on the Lewis and Clark pattern of the day. You'll feel better about portaging your canoe after seeing this one! Perhaps you'll reward your arrival at the 1000 mile mark with a few days off in Bismarck, the capital of North Dakota, but a smallish friendly town of about 30,000.

LAKE OAHE (BISMARCK ND TO PIERRE SD)

Soon after Bismarck you'll be in a lake again -- indeed the same lake through the rest of North Dakota and most of the north-south trek through South Dakota. Oahe is more like a super-river, narrow and long, lined with green grazing land and increasingly on the left shore actual crops. However it would be a mistake to assume Oahe as an easy paddle. If the wind is right (or, rather, wrong) the waves will rise to three to four feet and even if you have two excellent paddlers, there are some days you can't stay even and will be wind bound. If you are solo and using a little kicker, you will seem so tiny, as you sit in the troughs and stare horizontally at the tops of the waves on either side of you. The trick is to make plenty of miles in this lakes when it is calm, then sit out the big windstorms.

But high waves perhaps won't be the greatest threat to your trek when you get to the endless

Lake Oahe. If you are trekking the entire Missouri River you will probably face a greater challenge: boredom. By now you will have become acclimated to life on the river. You'll be used to the open prairies, beautiful sunsets, wildlife, and picture-postcard scenes. The Bitterroot mountains, Great Falls, and conquering Ft. Peck lake are now a distant memory. Your thoughts will turn to St. Louis. You'll likely get out all your maps and try to predict a firm finish date. You'll start counting miles *downward* (to St. Louis) instead of upward (from your starting point in Montana). And you'll figure out some day after you've been on the river for more than a month that you still are only half way through!

Like marathon runners "hit the wall" and thru-hikers on the Appalachian Trail hit Pennsylvania and New York, you'll think your trek will never end. Trekkers in the "middle miles" of their journey often experience these doldrums. If you meet one you can see it in their glazed look. Experienced trekkers simply put it on "auto pilot" and eat up the miles of the middle section until the "countdown miles" look manageable again. It is in this middle section when trekkers often forget the date, or day, or even where they camped two nights ago... they just plod on, hoping the excitement will eventually return. Often journals dry up, and trekkers won't share with their partner how they feel, hoping secretly something will go wrong so they can go home. The "middle miles malaise" is something like homesickness.

If you come down with a case of this malaise, resist the urge to give up. Refuse to say, "it's not fun anymore" or "I've had enough." In a week or two you'll be through all the South Dakota lakes and around all the final dam portages, and you'll get your second wind. It is during the last third of the journey where your memory of the whole trip comes together. You'll remember vividly campsites and scenes from a thousand miles ago, and the whole trek will begin to find "convergence" in your mind, no longer running in sequence, but now remembered as a collage. This is trek "convergence." Jumping out early robs the trekker of this convergence experience. Better to simply go on auto pilot or take a week off when you get to Sioux City Iowa.

LAKE SHARPE
A sort of mini-Oahe, just 80 miles long, you'll clip through this lake faster, perhaps stopping in delightfully clean and neat Pierre, South Dakota's capital city, and at Lower Brule a "capital" of sorts of the reservation. The fascinating feature of the river (even though it is dammed up, everyone calls it "the river") on Lake Sharpe is the fantastic "Brule Big Bend." Here the river meanders in one gigantic 25 mile loop to return to the neck just 1 1/2 miles from where you were many hours before, or even a day earlier if the wind is wrong.

LAKE FRANCIS CASE
If you had the "middle miles malaise" you may lose it in this lake, where you'll pass the 1000 mile countdown mark. At Chamberlain, SD you'll float under I90 and figure you've got 969

miles left to St. Louis. Even though this lake extends 107 miles you'll be anxious to finish it (and the next shorter one) to be in the river un-dammed the rest of the way to St. Louis.

LEWIS AND CLARK LAKE/GAVINS POINT DAM

Your final lake is short and sweet -- just 30 miles long and the last dam portage of the journey -- even if you are continuing all the way to New Orleans, for from this point to St. Louis there are no dams, and even beyond that, there are locks for every dam.

SIOUX CITY

At Sioux City you'll really feel near the final run down the river. Here you'll likely see the river boat/museum which was dragged out of the river and perched on the shore. Maybe you'll take some time off to celebrate the end of the difficult waters of the lakes, and to catch your breath for the final push down the "channeled" all-river section to St. Louis. Maybe you'll stop off on the left shore to pay respects at the monument to Sergeant Floyd, the only loss of life on the Lewis and Clark trek. In all, when you leave Sioux City you should be refreshed for the final float down a faster-flowing river to St. Louis.

THE LOWER RIVER

From Sioux City to the mouth of the Missouri you'll be on totally different waters. The Missouri is easily divided into three kinds of water. About a third of the route runs through wild and natural river, largely undisturbed since Lewis and Clark traveled the river 200 years ago. A second third of the Missouri's route is through large lakes established by the Corps of Engineer's dams. Now you will enter the final third of the miles: the "industrial Canal" segment.

Here you'll run down the "channeled" Missouri where the current is swift and the channel narrow. You'll be thinking of St. Louis often, and you'll be ready to end this journey. Luckily that will be easier in the swift-running current where you'll often be able to double the miles you were accustomed to making each day on the lakes.

You'll see more towns now, and enjoy stopping off at the many river towns established by immigrants in the land rush era. You'll speed through the remaining 735 miles and soon reach the mouth of the Missouri just above St. Louis. By then you will have determined that the Missouri is really the main channel, and that the Mississippi is just one more river flowing into this mighty river which became a tributary of the other river only by a fluke of history.

Perhaps you'll determine to canoe the extra 15 miles to end your trek under the St. Louis arch, a monument to Westward expansion.

Though this lower river is less wild, it will serve you as an excellent transition back to ordinary life. Indeed, it will be during the lower river segment of the entire trek that you will experience "convergence" -- where the entire trek melds together into one experience in your memory.

And just hours after ending your trek, you'll be in an air conditioned automobile whisking home. At home, people will ask you all kinds of questions about your trek, which you'll dutifully answer, but there will be no way you can fully explain the incredible journey to them. You'll be worn out, and it may take weeks to recover. Physically, that is. For you will never "recover" otherwise from such a trek. You won't want to. It will soon have become so integrated into your self, that the trek will become part of who you will be for the rest of your life. And, you'll be forever grateful you took the risk to do it.

2

TREKKING GEAR

A helpful list of gear to take on your trek.

Some trekkers are "gear heads," constantly absorbed with their gear, always thinking if they had the "right" gear they'd be doing better. Gear is a necessity, but don't think it is critical. Trekkers with the finest gear drop out after a few days, and others with lousy gear make it all the way.

The following list is just to give you the idea of what one canoe trekker carried, and in no way reflects the "ideal list." The gear you carry (or leave behind) is your own personal decision. But perhaps another trekker's gear list might help remind you of things, so here goes.

BEDROOM
_1. Tent (Marmot "Screech" - a superb 1-2-man tent with a spacious porch)
_2. Sleeping bag (A 3-season bag through June 10, a summer bag after that... expect 40 degrees nights in Montana during May)
_3. Therm-a-rest self inflating sleeping pad. (Hey, I'm in my 50's)
_4. Therm-a-rester device to turn the pad into a chair-with-a-back (How one misses back support on a trek... I thought of using this in the canoe all day, but never got around to it.)
_5. Hygiene kit

- Toothbrush
- Roll-on deodorant (the lightest per protection)
- Disposable razor (the single blade works best in cold water)
- Hand cream (if you get dry cracking hands in the outdoors)
- Pills (at least some Advil for "sun headaches."
- Soap (a motel bar is enough)
- Toilet paper (for its obvious use plus pot cleaning)
- Hand sanitizer (for after the obvious use of TP)
- Plastic shovel (also related to TP)
- After shave (well, you wouldn't have to I guess)

KITCHEN

_1. Stove. (I switched from my traditional backpacking loyalty from MSR to the French Butane Camping-gaz stove -- a bit heavier but 100% cleaner and quieter)

_2. Pot.   Early on, I dumped my hard-to-clean aluminum pot and picked up a one-quart Teflon lined saucepan, which, when the pretty wooden handle was removed was light enough, and surely much easier to clean. I used a folded piece of tin foil for a lid. I ate out of the pot, of course, being alone.

_3. Water jug. You can drink the river if filtered or treated. The sewage can be filtered or treated. But I wasn't too excited about drinking the herbicide-pesticide cocktail for two months and was sure chlorine wouldn't fix it, and unsure if filtering would. So I carried a 5 gal. Hard-sided water jug which was replaced by a collapsible 2 1/2 gallon jug later.

_4. Food. More than any one item you carry, your food pack will be determined by your taste... literally. My example:

> Breakfast: Pop tarts, bagels, Tang, (or Steak and eggs if arriving at a town before noon!)
>
> Lunch: Bagels, Peanut butter and Jelly sandwiches, Deviled ham on crackers, Kool Aid. But frankly I usually skipped lunch.
>
> Dinner: Mac & Cheese, Lipton meals, Mac & Cheese, Rice-a-roni meals, Mac & Cheese, and... Mac & Cheese.

OFFICE/LIBRARY
_1. Writing kit. Pens, paper, stamped envelopes, postcards, postcard stamps, e-mail device, palmtop computer.

2. Maps. I used the regular DeLorme state road atlas maps, tearing out the pages and re-numbering them in the proper sequence before leaving. These are expensive (nearly $100 if you get the whole river) but, for my preferences they were quite suitable. I prefer a map which has "a day's travel" on one or two sheets (I had 49 maps and took 47 days to complete my trek), I hate to fool around with maps all day,

especially when it is raining. The Delorme maps had GPS data on them and were fine. But if you want to know right where you are at all times, you may want the more detailed maps the DeLorme mapping software produces, or geological maps. I use a map to see what major thing I should look for next... a bridge, a town, a giant bend, and care little about knowing exactly where I am in between. And, if I get lost, I take a GPS reading and plot it on the map.

_3. Books. See the book list in this guide for suggestions, I took Lewis & Clark's Journals to read, and a Bible. (A wind bound day or two will have you reading Lipton directions and tea bag tags if you don't take books along.) Perhaps I went overboard, but I carried as much as 20 pounds of books at a time, rotating some in and out by mail.

WARDROBE
_1. Pants & shirt (Columbia nylon-poly - can be washed out and put back on wet and will dry in 20 minutes.)
_2. Tee shirt. (Patagonia Capalene. easy to wash, dries in 10 minutes, does not retain odor. But expensive.)
_3. Undershorts. Standard K-Mart brand running shorts.
_4. Fleece. (May/Montana)
_5. Gore-tex pants and jacket. (Not necessarily for the rain, but for the breakers crashing over/into your lap in the lakes.)
_6. Hat. (with beak as sunshade)
_7. Boots and Beach socks. (I needed boots for portaging and intended to wear beach socks in

the canoe. As it turned out I wore the boots all the time -- including walking in the water -- and used the beach socks as "camp slippers." However, I eventually traded both the boots and beach socks for one pair of sandals which was quite superior.

_8. Socks. (2 pr. smart-wool, one too many -- only needed for long walks into town.)

_9. Gloves. It seems silly to talk of gloves in 80 degree temperatures, but with 40 degree water crashing over you when the lakes are rolling, and when it clouds over, you'll be plenty grateful you brought them. I took a pair of "fleece" gloves with a set of Oregon Research Gore-Tex over-mittens. (though the mittens leaked after an hour of splashing from the waves and I wound up wearing the soaked fleece gloves for warmth after that).

DAY KIT
(It is frustrating to need something through the day but it is stowed away in the bottom of one of your Seal-line bags. The solution: a "day pack." I carried a soft pack (Seal-line) for jackets, etc. and an Old Town waterproof "ammunition box" with the following:

1. Cameras (Disposable...often one wide angle double size)
2. Sunglasses (darkened more than Wal-Mart Vision Center thinks is reasonable -- the sun shines down *and up* off the water. And, if you wear glasses, you'll need the regular ones too if you darken the sunglasses like you should (if you intend to enter a store while on the trek, that is.)
_3. Wallet and credit card.

_4. GPS (I thought a GPS was a luxury-toy until I navigated the giant lakes packed with side arms wider than the main channel. Not that I kept it running all the time, but it makes a good check every hour or so. And, when you've canoed four miles down an arm to find it dead ending, you can check and plot where you actually are!)
_5. Current map
_6. Water bottles (Gatorade or PowerAide bottles -- I drank two quarts through the day, and two at night. In later season you may need more.
_7. "P Bottle" (Hey, sometimes the shore is 4 miles away.)

DITTY/MISCELLANEOUS
_1. Thread/Needle
_2. Felt marker (I found the best way to hitch was mark a cardboard with "to town" on one side and "to river" on the other.
_3. Radio (if weather is important to you -- and it never will be more important than on this trek)
_4. Clothes pins (6)
_5. Insect repellent. (I never used mine, but it seemed like a good thing to take, given a reading of the Lewis and Clark journals.
_6. Laundry pen. (I write a running record of each campsite on the inside of my tent, supplying a constant past memory of all trips to recall when I've had too much coffee before bedtime)
_7. First aid kit. (at least Band-Aids and adhesive tape.)

_8. Duct tape. (wrapped around one water bottle -- to repair anything, including your boat.)
_9. Leatherman knife. (mine was a gift.)

BOAT ETC.
_1. Canoe. Ideally for this trek you'd have two boats. A narrow swift canoe for the river and a stable flat-bottomed skiff for the large lakes. Unable to take two, I chose a Grumman S-canoe, a hybrid of a square stern canoe and a skiff. It is an extremely stable craft, but weighs in at a bit over 100 pounds -- which is pretty hefty for a solo portage.

_2. Paddles. (even if you take a kicker, at least one)

_3. Canoe Cover. (Perhaps the best way to ensure yourself from swamping in the lakes. When your freeboard is 6" and the rollers are three feet, they will crash over the sides and swamp you in five minutes. I left the cover snapped down everywhere except right around me, effectively giving a Kayak appearance and security against the waves.)

_4. Flag. (a bicycle flag, primarily to give a festive look, but some usefulness in keeping an eye on the canoe down over the bank while camping. Most canoeists are always worrying that the river will somehow reach up at night and snatch away their canoe. To glance out the front door of the tent and see the orange flag flapping reassuringly was always a relief.)

_5. Bilge pump. (Aquateria, kayak pump. I needed a bilge pump even with the boat cover on the rough waters of the big lakes. Enough water still broke over the canvas top and crashed in through the small open space around me to produce several inches in the floor of my canoe in ten minutes, during high seas, and that was *before* my boat started leaking.)

_6. Sponge. (The pump can never get it all.)

_7. Line. (100' nylon line. I tied half to the stern, the other half to the bow and secured both at night. Sometimes the dams will raise the water level 2-3 feet at nights and a canoe merely pulled out on the shore is liable to wind up downstream the next morning if not firmly secured. Solid tie ups are often 50' from the shoreline.

_8. Car topper blocks. (I had to use them to get my canoe out to Montana; they were light, so I kept them in case I ever needed them if I rented another car.)

_9. Life vest. (I promised my wife to wear it every time I was on the water and kept my promise. I got so used to wearing it that I sometimes left it on when I went into town to re-supply... then noticed people glancing at me in a funny sort of way while in the Walmart line.)

_10. Portage pal. (If your canoe is portage-able on your shoulders, you won't need this. As a solo paddler, with a 100 pound canoe I did. It is a simple wheeled device manufactured by Hart

Designs to turn the canoe into a wheeled vehicle. When the portage may be a mile or more it is a great asset. I strapped the wheels under the bow, then raised the square stern to my tummy, and pushed the canoe wheelbarrow-like, carrying the weight of the stern on straps I rigged from the canoe up to a Kelty frame pack which carried the weight on my shoulders and transferred it to the large muscles of my legs. It was still awkward, but I found it better then hauling the canoe after me like a trailer.)

_11. Backpack frame. (For portaging the canoe primarily, but occasionally when leaving the canoe by the river, and hiking off to a distant campsite or hotel, I strapped several of my Seal-line bags on it to "make camp" in one trip.

IF USING A MOTOR.
_1. Motor. If you have a partner you don't need a motor. But if you are unable to persuade anyone to accompany you on your trek a little kicker for your canoe may make the difference between finishing the trek, and stalling part way through in frustration. The trek can be made solo by paddle, but you will need to allow three months to do it, perhaps longer. And if you do go solo and motor-less, you will be sorely tempted after such minor progress down some of the lakes to jump out and skip the lakes (more than 1/3 of the total miles).

I used a brand new Johnson five HP kicker, which (when run at quarter speed) gave me the "stern paddler" I needed to make it through the lakes. On the rivers I either paddled without the motor, or ran the motor at "partner speed" to keep moving. Though the river can run five to seven MPH in places, don't count on more then two MPH average current. To figure the current contribution to your speed simply float with your GPS running and read out the speed.

_2. Fuel cans (3) I started with four and set one free after coming through the wild and scenic/Ft. Peck section. Everywhere else I really only needed two, but kept the third as a cushion. My 5 HP Johnson gave me about 125 miles on the lakes per six-gallon tank, about 150 river miles. (However a strong lake head wind can cut the miles down to 100 per tank. In the lower river there are marinas on the lakes and river which makes fueling up far easier than toting the cans a few miles through town to a gas station. (However, people are more likely to pick you up with a gas can, perhaps thinking you've run out of gas somewhere, which is true in a way.)

_3. Two-cycle oil. While the marinas carry it (at a few dollars per pint!) the gas stations in little towns often do not. Don't forget to add it -- in all of the hubbub of a town trip it is easy to drop the can back in the canoe oil-less. The best trick is to always add the oil before stowing the cans back in the canoe, even in the rain. It may save you burning up your engine.

_4. Extra sheer pins. More than you'd expect -- I used a dozen or so on the first third of the journey, and a few more for the lower river's snags.

_5. Replacement parts. (Prop, Prop nut, fuel filter, gear lube, water pump.)

_6. Tool kit (Pliers, screw driver, mini-size WD-40)

_7. Poly tube. I took ten feet of 1/2" poly tubing to siphon gas from cars under the premise that cars are easier to find than gas stations. Of course, one asks first.

3

TIPS AND HINTS

Ideas, tips, and good hints from veterans trekkers.

GROUPS & EDUCATION

The Missouri River is an ideal location for a "Floating Classroom" educational experience. However remember that floating down the river *per se* is not education. Experience is not education. The trick to turning a wonderful experience into an educational enterprise is the outside reading you require, the discussions you facilitate, and the follow-up project selected. These transform experience into education.

Each year Tom Nielson leads a "Floating Classroom" program out of Northern Montana College using a raft and pull-along boat. Groups can make the learning experience in canoes or rafts, with or without land support. While the Lewis and Clark journeys might be the primary focus of such trips, much wider subject areas are also relevant, for a trek down the Missouri is like making an archeological trench across an ancient tell. It turns up information on geology, biology, sociology, paleontology, along with the historical findings related to Westward expansion, the land rush and the immigrant's, native American issues, and, of course, the Lewis and Clark expedition.

LAKE TRAVEL

Most trekkers underestimate the number, size and danger of the lakes. Be prepared to negotiate a surf of two feet or more and plan in your supplying to automatically figure in several days of being "wind bound." The lakes are often more remote than the river sections, so count of being away from people, phones and supplies several days or more at a time.

RIVER TRAVEL

The river sections (about two thirds of the trip) will likely be your favorite segments, especially the Wild and Scenic" river sections. The Missouri is a swift river and helps you get down it. (Unless, of course, you are going upstream, which then changes the sentence to "The Missouri fights your progress with a swift current which will some days seem insurmountable.")

CAMPSITES

In Montana and the Dakotas you can camp just about anywhere, including at the landing sites. If you are near a ranch house you should ask, but much of the open range is far from the house and appears to be unsettled. As you move past the ranches into the farm land of Nebraska, Iowa, and Missouri open shoreline campsites are harder to find, especially if the river is flooding. The tops of the levees often offer the only adequate open spots. However, in the lower river there are far more public and private campgrounds, so the number of sites is actually not diminished. While "fishing cabins" are almost non-existent in the upper river, there are many in the lower river offering "yards" for a tent site. If asked, few fishermen will turn you down.

MISSOURI SILT & A MOTOR

If you decide to use a motor or "kicker" to help you down the river, be prepared to burn up the water pump by the constant pumping of the silt-filled water. While this is exacerbated below Sioux City where there are no dams to settle out the silt and sand, it is then multiplied again during flood conditions, which are common on the lower Missouri in July. If you are not comfortable with replacing your own water pump, be ready to arrange for its replacement somewhere in the lower Missouri.

GOOD 500+ MILE TREKS

Canoe Trekking is generally considered to be a journey of 500 or more miles. Using that criterion there are several great partial treks on the Missouri:

1. Montana   More than 700 miles of river starting at Three Forks and winding through wild and scenic river sections, cliffs, fast flowing clear water, numerous dams, the Great Falls, and through several lakes to the confluence of the Yellowstone and the Missouri at the north Dakota border. A delightful 700+ mile trek which would be my own first choice to repeat.

2. Sioux City to St. Louis
The lower 735 miles of channeled river where you travel with the barge traffic on fast flowing

current with frequent towns marinas and historical spots to stop and visit and no dams to portage. An easy trip for motored travel.

3. The Dakotas
While there are river sections in this thousand mile middle section, it is primarily made up of narrow lakes and would be ideal for lake trekking, especially with a sea-worthy boat.

MAPS AND NAVIGATION CHARTS
The new DeLorme software might provide the best help, though there are several other map sources you might want to add:

1. The Upper Missouri Wild and Scenic River maps set. (Map 1&2 together and map 3&4 together on waterproof Tyvek) Available from Bureau of Land Management, Lewistown District, Airport Road, Lewistown Montana, 59457

2. Missouri River Navigation Charts. There are two sets of navigation charts produced for barges by the U S Army Corps of Engineers: *Sioux City to Kansas City*, and *Kansas City to the mouth*. Each includes more than 70 sequential color charts of every detail imaginable which might be important to barge traffic. That, however is the hitch. They are for barges, and are not very trekker-friendly (though they are increasingly under pressure to make them so, and have recently included more campsite and marina information). These chart sets are available from either of the district offices:

US Army Corps of Engineers
District Office
215 North 17th Street
Omaha, Nebraska 68102-4978

OR

US Army Corps of Engineers
District Office
700 Federal Building
Kansas City MO 64106-2896

While you may purchase these before entering the lower river, consider that the charts are so detailed that you will have to switch to the next chart every ten or twenty minutes if the current is running fast. Since they are so detailed as to be almost unusable (especially in the rain) consider not making the purchase, and stopping at one of the Corps on-river offices where you can often get them for free by asking the field officer.

3. Corps lakes recreational maps.

If you are canoeing the entire river, contact the Omaha office and also ask for the following free Corps recreational maps. Though they are inadequate for navigation, they do supply important campground, access and marina details.

- Ft. Peck Lake (Ft. Peck Dam)
- Lake Sakakawea (Garrison Dam)
- Lake Oahe (Oahe Dam)
- Lake Sharpe (Big Bend Dam)
- Lake Francis Case (Ft. Randall Dam)
- Lewis & Clark Lake (Gavins Pt. Dam)

CURRENT
The Missouri is a fast-flowing river. The Corps of Engineers used to have a sign at the mouth warning boaters that the river was unsuitable for recreational boating and full of snares, wing dams and dangerous currents. The message: stay away, this river is reserved for barges. The most common pleasure boat guidebook did not even list the lower Missouri for years. However boaters have learned to negotiate these more difficult currents. It is true that the Missouri has a fast-flowing current. The average fall of the Missouri River is twelve times greater than the Mississippi. So this river seems in a hurry to tumble down to the sea. In July when the major snow melt hits river it is commonly at flood stage and may run at five to seven miles per hour.

However, don't imagine you will be able to simply sit on the river and float 60 miles in ten hours. The channel current wanders all across the river bed leaving much of the river floating at less than a mile an hour, and sometimes running backwards up the inbanks. Even floating the current will take full time work to stay in the current.

HITCHING A RIDE.
Sooner or later you'll have to hitch into town, unless you want to combine canoe trekking with hiking. The tips for hitching are simple:

<u>1. Use a sign.</u> A simple all-purpose sign says "To Town" on one side and "To River" on the other. If you are going longer distances, the

specific name of the town is even better. When desperate simple write "please?" on one side...

2. Carry something in your hands. Not a full pack (if you can help it) but at least something recognizable (a small cooler is ideal, as is a gas can).

3. Take off your hat and sunglasses, they pick up your face, remember.

4. Open up your jacket if you have one... appear open.

5. For pickup trucks use your finger in a curling gesture indicating that you are willing to ride in the back. (this willingness often gets you up front anyway.)

6. Two get rides easier than one. Take a friend.

7. A woman and a man is an "auto-ride."

8. Pick a good place. Either a startup spot or a place where there is plenty of pull-off room.

9. Don't be afraid to ask. If you are at a gas station or parking lot, simply ask. People often will help another person out if they are asked point blank.

10. Don't expect rides with women alone. Once I see a woman driving, I simply smile and wave, dropping my thumb and sign. (which ironically sometimes gets me a ride with the woman anyway -- mostly grandmotherly type women.)

GETTING HELP AROUND THE DAMS.

You can portage all 14 if you want to, but giving people a chance to help provides them with the opportunity to share in your trip and they always go away feeling good about their service -- it is a win-win situation. The tips:

<u>1. Ask.</u> Wait for a fisherman or somebody with a pickup and simply ask them.

<u>2. Let them off the hook.</u> Don't be insistent -- just offer them the chance to serve. If they refuse, say, "no problem.. I'll find somebody." (On my entire trek I only had one outright refusal.. a fellow about 45, beautifully tanned, with a gold chain around his neck and gold link bracelet on his wrist -- and a blonde about 30 waiting on his boat which he'd already launched... I shoulda' known better than to have even asked!)

<u>3. Use the word "help."</u> As in, "Would you HELP me by taking me around the dam before you park?"

<u>4. Tell them what you're doing.</u> After a short pause say, "I'm canoeing to St. Louis" (or wherever).

<u>5. Then shut up.</u> Don't over sell. Let them make up their mind.

<u>6. Follow the hitching rules for dress</u> (take off hat & sunglasses, open jacket).

7. <u>As a last resort</u> (if they him and haw) offer to pay. But be careful doing this -- most people (especially on vacation) would rather help a stranger than get paid.

8. <u>Thank them profusely</u> as soon as you are in the truck.

9. <u>En route tell them about your trip.</u> Don't worry, they'll interview you.

10. <u>Thank them again</u> when you are arriving at the put-in site.

11. <u>Get their name and address</u> once you get to the put-in site. Ask, "Can I send you a card letting you know when I finish - you sure helped me along."

12. <u>Write a postcard</u> to them the next day thanking them again.

13. <u>Send them another postcard</u> before you finish. This allows them to vicariously participate in your trek. You will discover that more than half of the men who carry you around the dams have dreamed of doing some sort of trek like you are doing. Few ever will actually do it. Your contact with them allows them to live through your trek, and it is the least service you can give back to them Some of these helpers will post every one of your cards above their workbench, leaving them there for years to come.

14. <u>When finished send a final note or gift.</u> If you've kept a journal and type it up, send them a

signed copy. Other trekkers get a slew of pictures made and sign them, sending them to all their helpers. Still others go back through their notes the following Christmas and send a picture-card once again thanking their helpers. Remember... there are other trekkers coming along behind you. Make every person who helps you glad they did.

4

My own day-by-day Trekking Journal

The author of this guidebook took the Missouri River Trek in 1999. Sometimes it helps to read another trekker's journal in making your own trek. The following is the trek journal from May-July 1999.

May 18, (At Three Forks, Montana)

I am snuggled up in my Marmot tent as a gusty rain storm sweeps over me this afternoon, Tuesday May 18... I just made it to Three Forks Montana and grabbed some groceries from one of those stores run "just right" (i.e. *"NO ! You can't have that box -- it's my baked good box!."* "But the butcher said I could." *"The butcher doesn't know what he's doing -- here, give me that box."* No, he said I could have it." *"You want me to call the sheriff?"* Surrendering her precious box, I packed up my groceries in a paper sack, and sneaked away as if I'd been caught shoplifting.

I had always wondered what happened to nurse Rratchet from One Flew Over -- now I find her running a grocery store in Three forks Montana!

My campsite is directly on the three forks which join to make the Missouri. Across from me are cliffs rising 300' from the other side of the river. The river is smaller than I expected. I'll be scraping unless they have some good warm sun melting the snow-covered peaks to my West.

The leaves are just breaking out... unfolding but not dense enough that you can't see through each tree. Tomorrow (Wed.) I'll return the car to Helena 70 mi. North of here then hitch back and [probably] cast off in the afternoon or Thursday morning.

Right now everything is here in my tent while thunder crashes about me... and I'm going to organize my gear before going to sleep.

May 19, (to Townsend, Montana)

I awoke to such thick fog I could not even see *my* side of the river, just 20' away, let alone the other side. Drove the 75 miles to Helena & dropped off my rental car at the airport, which I had used to carry all my gear and canoe from Indiana the week before today. Took a $7 taxi ride back to Rt. 2 and started hitching back to Three Forks. The second guy along picked me up, a local painter and took me 5 miles. I found a piece of cardboard and wrote "Three Forks" on it with my black marker and within 5 minutes Barry Brown a salesman for medical supplies picked me up. He had never seen the Three Forks, so he took me all 70 miles right back to my tent and boat, so I was packed up an on the water heading down the Missouri River by noon.

All day I played leapfrog with a father-son kayak team... they passed me once when I broke a sheer pin and had to paddle to shore to replace it. Again while I was portaging the too-many-items-I-brought around the Toston Dam, they past me with their lightweight kits. They hung around for a snack and I made 15 more miles before shearing another pin in yet another rapids -- I only have two left so I better get deeper water soon, or learn to read the river better.

Since I had to pull out to repair the shear pin, and it was already 6 PM, I decided to camp -- about an hour before Canyon Ferry Lake. It is kind of funny to be traveling north -- even a bit *northwest* on my way to St. Louis. But the river here travels north until Great Falls where it turns east, and finally over in North Dakota it will turn south. This was discouraging to Lewis and Clark who were coming upstream heading west -- and they encountered this southern and eastern section of river. (Coming back they cut off this loop, of course.)

It is sunny, the sky is blue, and I've seen Pelicans, Cormorants, prairie dogs, King birds, Great Blue Herons, Canada geese, and scores of ducks I can't identify yet.

Tonight's campsite is perched 20' above the water...the sun is warming my back and I'm about to cook the ever-present mac & cheese dinner. A good start!

May 20 , (to Kim's Marina, Montana)
N 46-39.060   W 111-42.017

A frustrating day which ended well. Within a mile of my campsite I hit a rock and sheared another pin...didn't even replace it but paddled the rest of the way to Townsend bridge. But in the silence I coasted by three Mule Deer nibbling bushes on the shore, then a pair of eagles standing guard in a high tree.

Hitched into Townsend chasing down more shear pins, but none were available. At the little NAPA store Ed, a 75 year old retired Meter reader, overheard my request and hauled me home to give me a shear pin from his 1952 Evenrude -- "they're all the same," he assured me before taking me back to my canoe. (they aren't).

Afraid of shearing my second last pin, I simply paddled the next 5 miles into Canyon Ferry Lake before powering up and heading for Goose Bay Marina half way up the 5-mile wide lake, feeling stupid for coming on this trek with only a handful of shear pins and absolutely frustrated at even having to bring a motor along.

A motor isn't needed if one is canoeing with a partner, but becomes pretty necessary for a solo trip, especially across the lakes and all the giant waves. I did not have the three months free to make the entire trek motor-less, and was unwilling to sit on the shores of the big lakes for several days at a time out waiting the wind, so I tossed in this motor as my "partner." Like most partners, it is a blessing and a curse. The breaking of shear pins is the curse part.

No dice. At least no sheer pins. All Goose Bay marina offered was pleasant retired Elizabeth who sold potato chips, not shear pins: "To tell you the truth I don't know what one is" she confessed. I checked everything in the bait store and sure enough, they had none.

Tired of shear pin chasing, I headed for the North end of the lake were Elizabeth said the "better type of people" kept their boats.

Jacking up my speed to maximum I started racing (well, this little kicker doesn't exactly enable me to "race" but I usually run it at a bit above idle speed -- so it contributes about the same energy as my wife would, though it is quite a bit more noisy than she). A gigantic rainstorm is coming in from the west. Remembering the warning about this lake and its sudden 70 MPH winds and 20' rollers, I clung to the shore to run for cover if I saw lighting.

However, I made it. Kim's Marina, indeed a place for a "better type of people." At least better off. I got a tent site for $10. and a shower for $2 then walked up the hill to "Butch's Marine," an out-of-the-garage operation seeking my shear pins. "Sure, I got everything you need," he grinned recovering a greasy box from the shelf and dumping out a hundred shear pins, of fifty different sizes. Searching through them he found five near-matches: "You might have to file 'em down, but these'll work."

I am now at O'Malley's Irish Pub where I just finished the "Cowboy Classic" including a delicious "Indian Pan Bread" which seems to be a doughnut without the sugar -- and it is superbly delicious!

As I was eating the storm hit-- and I saw those rollers and whitecaps they warn about. I was glad I made it. The storm is now passed and the sunset is beautiful. I am headed to bed with a hamburger steak in my tummy and five shear pins in my pocket-- what more could a fella' ask for?

Perhaps that's the wonder of this simple life -- it doesn't take much to make your day!

May 21 (to Gates of the Mountains)
I got an early start to Canyon Ferry dam portage...straight up a shale bank 90' to the road, then over a 5' concrete wall & down 400 or more feet of rock slide/"trail". Asking the dam workers for help, one wanted to haul me around in his pick up truck, but when he called his dam supervisor the response was, "That's his problem, not ours." I worked two hours inching the boat up the shale slide with two ropes when one knot slipped and the whole boat went slamming and sliding all the way back down the crumbling shale KER-SPLASHING right back into the lake!

I said phooey, tossing everything back into the canoe and went to a boat launch a mile back. There Pete & Hank were just unloading their boat for a day of fishing and they agreed to haul me round the 5 miles by road. For forty dollars, that is. I would have paid more. (Later note: This was the only "paid portage" I made -- from this point on everyone happily agreed to portage me for free, sometimes even giving me food or other gifts. I was still a rookie at Canyon Ferry Dam.)

There! The portage is out of the way! Well, that one... soon came the next dam -- Hauser Dam. Sneaking past the limit cable to avoid another tobogganing boat folly, I exited the water 10' from the dam, hauled everything up to the road where there was a gradual 600' gravel road around the dam. A much better portage than Canyon Ferry. Then along came Todd and Guy, the dam managers, who drove over the dam tossed everything in their truck and hauled the whole kit around for me. What wonderful fellows!

Then down five mile of *rapids*...amazing... I could see the river falling away just like a long downhill interstate and I rode down this "hill" on two foot waves in good spirits. Exciting!

But I must have been tense. I rested at Gates of the Mountains Boat club (a place where regular auto-tourists can take tour boats into the Gates). And I am weary. Today features a perfectly blue sky, with 70 degrees and beautiful sunshine!

Camped for the night down in the "Gates of the Mountains" a 500 foot deep gorge through the foothills of the rocky mountains. I camped at the delightful Colter campsite, a canoe-in back country site on a shelf of grass deep in the canyon. (N46-51.563 W11-54.500)

Lewis & Clark had heard of the "Gates of the Mountains" a thousand mile before from the Indians. When they arrived they rejoiced that they would soon pass through the "Gates" and begin seeing snow capped mountains. The opposite was true for me -- I was bidding the snow capped peaks goodbye.

May 22 (to Cascade Montana).
Awakened by geese roostering in the dawn, I decided to wait 'till the sun hit the top of the canyon wall across the river. Then I hit the mental snooze alarm and chose half way down the wall.

The sun now illuminates the opposite shoreline and I am making my second pot of tea! Oh well, the only schedule to keep is a half-way meeting with Sharon in 21 days and 1100 miles...I'll make it up ;-)

Leaving later than normal I canoed out of the "Gates" and up Holter Lake to stop at the "Boat Loft" a first class marina opposite Holter Dam, for a half-dozen cups of free coffee (and another half-dozen shear pins which their mechanic supplied for me happily.) They promised me the Holter Dam portage is not so bad. Of course they've never actually portaged it themselves -- just looked at it from the lake.

It is a cold morning -- I now have on every bit of clothes I brought including both sets of gloves.

I portaged around Holter dam, with the help of Steve and Paula Western of Great Falls who were taking a day off to wander around the water. They along with their three friends, hand-carried all my gear to the put-in site. I carried the canoe and discovered a better way to use the "Portage Pal" wheels -- I put the bow & wheels in *front* of me and lift the stern against my belly looping a rope over my shoulders to my Kelty frame pack -- it is considerably better than dragging the canoe behind like a trailer. This method is more like a wheel barrow. Steve & Paula gave me their phone number offering to help me in Great Falls if I needed it.

Well there was just one hitch. I selected the shortcut put-in site which had a 40' shale slide to get all my gear down to the water after Steve and Paula left. The canoe I inched down with two ropes. For the gear I rigged up a line to a tree at the river side and sent the rest of my gear (except the motor) down the rope --- pulley-like... slick!

I floated-paddled most of the next 15 miles roaring through Wolf Creek Canyon motor-less. Wolf Canyon is essentially a 15 mile long class two rapids! It was *exciting*! I couldn't use the motor anyway in rocky rapids - and the workout is good for me.

A fun ride, but tense. I pulled in as soon as I hit the valley and made camp on the right bank at

N47-11.500 W111-47.892. I am writing the name of each campsite on my new Marmot tent. I called this one "Rattlesnake #1 camp." Guess why?

May 23 (to Great Falls Island)

The fast water is gone now. Here the river winds, oozing slowly, meandering here and there, first north, then east, then south... one gets dizzy trying to follow the route to closely.

I stopped at Cascade to attend church, but only the two bars were open for business and the C-store. Hank, a C-store hanger-on assured me, "there's grizzly bears in that section 'tween here and Great Falls --you wouldn't catch me going down there." I suspected Hang didn't go much of anywhere... except the Cascade C-Store.

On to Ulm for some backup gas (One tank goes about 100-125 miles -- I started with two full tanks in 3 Forks) After walking to the station a toothless skinny guy said, "That your boat down by the bridge?" I admitted it was and he replied, "'Wanna ride back with that gas can?" Jeff was pumping water out of the river into a 500 gal plastic tank chained to a trailer "to water ma' trees -- well water ain't good for 'em, ya know."

Back on the meandering river until sunset. The river is often shallow here offering up hidden sand bars. However, these aren't as likely to shear the pin. At about sunset I arrived in Great Falls, camping on a sand bar near a large city-owned island right in the downtown. N47-29.045 W111-19.097

Tomorrow I plan rent a truck or car to portage around the series of Great Falls, though it took Lewis and Clark a month to do it 200 years ago. I think I will also take a day off for laundry, shopping, mailing home excess baggage and resting.

May 24 (at Great Falls, day off)
Canoed the short distance to the "second bridge" in Great falls and arranged for a U-Haul truck rental, tossed all my gear aboard, rented a $42 room at the Day's Inn; I re-packed my gear, did laundry-in-the-tub (and put my wet clothes right back on to wear 'em dry). I got two rolls of film developed at the Walmart 1-hour (for free it turned out, since it took 1 hour and 15 minutes, and I happened to mention it.)

Sent home several of the extra books I brought and had already read. After all, how may book does one actually need on a river trek? Answer: *more* when packing, *less* while portaging. Visited the "Giant Spring" just below Black Eagle falls/dam -- the largest spring in the world, gushing out 134,000 gallons per minute. They also claim it is the shortest river in the world sine it technically runs about 25' before entering the Missouri.

The Great Falls themselves are actually a series of falls dropping a total of 512 feet (for comparison Niagara drops a measly 150'). Lewis and Clark took a month to portage around them. The "Interpretive center" is a must-see but "never on a Monday" -- only ServiceMaster gets inside on Mondays.

Having completed all my errands, and soon to enter 300+ miles of wilderness, I treated myself to the new Star Wars movie and slipped into bed between fresh clean sheets for a night.

May 25, (to Rowe Bend)
(A day totally missing from my journal, but reconstructed afterward as the day I was met by Jim and Diane McDermond and taken to Carter landing, then canoed through Ft. Benton to camp somewhere in the Wild and Scenic river, my own map indicating somewhere near Rowe Bend.)

May 26 (to Judith Landing)
Hard going all morning against the wind. I had to run my little kicker-helper to fight a powerful head wind. It made me wonder what the giant lakes will be like -- especially Ft. Peck lake, soon to appear. However, by noon the wind died down and I made it all the way to Judith landing, 84 miles below Ft. Benton.

The only trouble: I gulped down 6 gal. fuel...and will not make it to Ft. Peck with the remaining fuel.

Then up comes Ethel & Robert Glover, vacationing Canadians ending a 3-day canoe trip. They hauled me and a tank 37 miles to the nearest crossroads - a town of about 100. The gas station was closed, but there was a guy filling up at a special pump at the side -- he gave me 4 gallons -- enough to take the pressure off and get me to Ft. Peck.

Then Robert & Ethel insisted on buying me a square meal at the so-called "restaurant" in the tiny town. I ate a 3/4 pounder.

They hauled me and my gas (both in my can and in my belly now) back to Judith Landing where I pitched my tent in the final glimmer of light.

It is now 10 PM and I just finished half of Ethel's 3/4 pounder she couldn't finish, keeping the tin foil it was wrapped in to use for a pot cover in the future, having forgotten mine from home.

May 27 (to Kipp Landing)

After last night's hamburger I determined to make a big day of it today. Up before dawn and off down river just at first light. I stopped at the one-car ferry and chatted with Grace Sanford a 70ish woman who is the ferryman. She was taking her own truck across to do laundry at a nearby ranch. "Beats bringing that old washer down here to the river," she said. We jawboned a hour before I broke away. Until recently Grace taught school in the winter, "Had three students, but one went to high school and another one moved away."

Hit a submerged rock and popped another shear pin and worse, when I jerked around my little radio went overboard and now I have no country music to accompany me. I'll have to make up my own ballads about dogs, pick up trucks, love and whiskey. Oh well, I was getting weary of the two stations anyway: one with the grain prices continuously interspersed with on-air want-ads. The other was a Christian station having their "friend-raising" week.

Made it to Kipp Landing (Frank Robertson Bridge) after 11 hours straight. From here it in only another 10 miles of river to the big lake -- Ft. Peck Lake then things could get mighty interesting!

May 28 (to Devil's Landing, Ft. Peck Lake)
Canoed 15 miles into the Ft. Peck Lake, and faced exciting rollers a couple feet high but knowing of the impending storm over Memorial Day weekend I kept at it all day and got 60% down the 134 mile lake to Devil's Creek campground where there are several fishermen camped. (A new family just drove their pickup in and did a walkabout just below me, and having seen two rattlesnakes got back in their pickup and drove off.)

I was lonesome today.

May 29 (at Devil's Creek; storm-bound)
Sure enough the storm rolled in by 10 PM. I had to run to the lake and better secure my canoe, the pounding three foot surf was knocking it to pieces.

Read and rested in my tent all day. Watched the rivulets of rain run down the fly for a break.

Retyped all my E-mail when the machine suddenly reset again. Read Lewis and Clark journals, Patrick Gass journals, and am hoping for a break in the storm tomorrow.

(The fishermen have spent most of the day sitting in their three pickup trucks with their heaters and radios on.)

May 30 (to Pine point-Ft. Peck lake)
An incredible day! Woke to the same threatening sky, but the water was glass-calm! I tossed everything together, gobbled down a strawberry toast-em and headed down-lake.

It was just a trick to get me on the water...soon the wind was roaring again and I found myself on two and three foot rollers. That's not so bad a sea -- except that my gunwales are only 6" high when I'm loaded. This day I was grateful for "Captain Bob's" contribution to my trip: the waterproof snap-on boat cover -- without it I would have capsized.

As it was, the bow dived into the next roller and the wave broke over the boat, washing in around me. Every ten minutes I would get out my bilge pump and pump furiously to drain the 3" of water at my feet.

I made it to the most delightful campsite of the trip so far. A pine covered narrow jut of land just 10 miles above the dam. All my clothes are now dried out, and I am in my tent just a few yards from my boat on the shore. The front door offers a complete vista of tomorrow's route. The water is calming a bit, the sun peeps through occasionally and I have tremendous sense of well being.

May 31 (to Ft. Peck, Montana)

A short 10 miles to finish the lake then I met a local couple at the marina who put my canoe on their trailer and hauled me the 4 miles down to the put-in site. Re-packed and secured canoe, then backpacked the mile or so back to "town" to stay at the WPA-style hotel.

Mike let me do my laundry in the hotel laundry, and I took a long bath in the ancient cast iron tub. The town of Ft. Peck once had 30,000 people in the 1930's when they were building the dam. It now has 300, a 99% shrinkage. After my delicious bath I walked the 4 miles to the Gateway Inn for a steak celebrating my coming 550 miles and finishing the most remote 300 miles of the entire river. I met and talked more than an hour with the 80ish "Sis Bondy" the oldest resident of Ft. Peck. Having moved here in the 30's, she told me stories about the dam not published in official journals.

I rested in the lodge-type atmosphere of the hotel, winding up the day on its rambling porch watching a half dozen mule deer graze on the lawn 50' away before retiring to my 1930-deco room.

June 1 (to Oswego -- a tiny island)
The period bed in the hotel of course sagged like all good beds did in the 30's. After sleeping on the ground for a few weeks I couldn't take it -- I got out of bed and slept on the floor.

Following a delightful breakfast with Clyde Allen and Brian Nohr of the Corps of Engineers I picked up my mail (including many letters, cards and even some cookies from my wife, and brownies from "Grasshopper" a fellow trekker from the Appalachian Trail years before) hoisted my pack and walked to the put-in site. There I found my canoe in good shape as I left it.

Two retired ladies met me on the way -- Edythe and Genell Herd and walked me to the launch site and saw me off. (Edyth and her husband stopped their gigantic motor home in the middle of the road yesterday, picking me up after the steak dinner saving me the 4 mile walk back to town).

Putted along slowly seeking my way through the shallow river to Oswego, and a few miles more to the most delightful grassy tiny island. Perhaps 50' round, as soon as I spied it I determined to make camp: "There's an island that needs camped on," I said.

As I write this the sun is sinking in the west. My canoe is a few yards out my front door and sitting on the bow of it is a brightly colored Baltimore Oriole chirping goodnight to me. Tomorrow I shall provision at Wolf Point for the trip to the confluence/Williston.

June 2 (to Poplar Montana - Bonepile CS)
Pulled into Wolf Point Montana by ten AM and was met near the sewage treatment plant (where they were fishing) by three Indian boys who offered to watch my canoe while I was in town (for an unspecified fee and with a specified threat: "las' guy came here got his boat stole.")

Picked up my first groceries and gas since Ft. Benton 300+ miles back, paid my five bucks ransom, then got back in the river The river is still shallow and filled with gravel bars, sometimes with only a 10' wide channel in a 200 yard. wide river, usually near the shore.)

Fought a 30 MPH head wind with 50 MPH gusts until 3 PM then tossed it in and made camp before the threatening thunderstorm caught me. My site is just before Poplar MT -- on the left shore beside a curious pile of bones, apparently from a steer who met his fate here. Who piled them up and why I can't guess. But they do decorate my front yard, like people put those plastic flamingos on their lawn to advertise they've been to Florida. I kind of like 'em -- sort of says, "See here what happened to the last fellers' who tried to shake me down for watching my canoe while I was in town?"

I have not seen a boat or shoreline fisherman since Ft. Peck - this is a remote section, even though the river passes several towns. The towns apparently do not think of the river in recreational ways for there are no docks or landing spots. They rather think of the river as a good place to put their sewage. For this reason I carry my own water most of the time. That, and the herbicide-pesticides in the Missouri from runoff is enough to convince me to carry my own water.

In Wolf Point I bought a $10 kid's play radio which is built right into earphones with an antenna sticking out the top. When I wear it I look somewhat like a Martian. The radio provides some company at least (besides, of course my bonepile.)

Sure enough, the thunder & lighting are coming at 9 PM. I'm crawling in to my sleeping bag now.

June 3 (to Culbertson bridge)
(A day totally missing from my journal which I recollected later as being a day with numerous tornado warnings on the radio to which I responded by canoeing to Culbertson Bridge and set up my tent under the massive concrete bridge.)

June 4 , 1999 (to Lewis and Clark State Park)
Sure enough, according to my tiny radio, there were six tornado touchdowns last night, so my makeshift tornado cellar under the Culbertson Bridge was a wise decision. But I personally saw no storm evidence anywhere, other than wind and rain.

I wiggled back and forth down the still-shallow Missouri to the reconstructed Ft. Union which once was directly on the river, but now boasts a serious marsh between it and the river, through which I tried to find a route. I failed. In a later visit (during my weekend off in Bismarck) the fort was a satisfying site, though the management of this National Monument is short-sighted in wanting to "avoid the trouble" of river visitors. Ironic, isn't it -- river visitors is what the fort was all about originally. Now extravagant expenses are shelled out for parking areas and handicapped accessibility. But for

Lewis and Clark trekkers, not even a dozen loads of gravel for a footpath can be invested. Perhaps it is a commentary on what has happened to America's rivers -- they are now the sewers, and the new rivers are the highways.

From the fort downstream, the river was being backed up from the flow of the swollen Yellowstone River. Crossing into North Dakota. I now have 770 miles behind me. That's "government miles" --more, if you count real miles -- the way the steamboats did.

At the confluence of the Yellowstone and Missouri I discovered that the Yellowstone was indeed at flood stage, pouring reddish muddy water which quickly dominated the more quiet and clear Missouri. This probably explains why the Missouri was so shallow. The dam boys may have been holding back the Missouri's flow to allow the Yellowstone water downstream. The Yellowstone runs largely unrestricted from the snow melt to the confluence.

Catching "Paddlefish" is big at the confluence. Some days 60-70 fish are caught. The large "Gold Star Caviar" company sets up shop during May and early June to clean the fish for free if they get to keep the roe. I looked for the Colorado plates to leave a note to the father-son kayak team who planned to finish their trek here, but could not find their car. I asked at the caviar trailer and was told, "Yeah, they came here in their Suburban with two kayaks on top about a week ago -- they gave up."

I wondered why. The storm on Canyon Ferry lake? The portage? Getting along as father and son. Simply satisfied that they'd done enough? I regretted not getting their address and figured I would never connect with them again now. (Later note: After my trek I received an e-mail from the father... they had made it to Ft. Benton and simply been satisfied that they'd gone far enough.

The caviar manager shook his head when I said I planned to go into Williston for supplies. "It won't work. You'll never find your way in -- I'll give you gas right here" and he promptly supplied all my needs for the next 200 miles out of the Gold Star tanks and pocketed the cash (probably to be turned in later, I'm sure).

Sure enough, I soon discovered why he was sure I'd not get into Williston. The "Williston Marsh" is a tangled spaghetti bowl of turnouts, streams, dead ends, and ox bows. I finally gave up figuring out where I was and just kept going downstream, first with the sun in my face, then on my right ear, then my back, and then in my face again. A couple hours later I emerged into beautiful Lake Sakakawea, relieved to be out of the marsh.

I was looking for "Lund's Landing," a little fish restaurant I had been taken to quite a few years before as a visiting speaker in Williston. I wound up in the wrong bay, tied up my boat and walked into the back yard of Dick and Linda Hickman asking for directions. Linda is the DA for Williston, and Dick had just received a call to serve a year's stint as a peace keeper for the

UN in Kosovo (just this week the bombing had stopped). They welcomed me into their home and served me supper. Linda took a glance at my "outdoored" hands and said gently, "I'll put out a towel and washcloth for you." Wonderful people!

Now knowing the way to Lund's Landing, but no longer needing to go for dinner, I put in at Lewis and Clark State park where they have boat-in/walk-in campsites.

The rest of the evening was spent talking with ranger Sheila Koerner who was trained in veterinary medicine, then worked for an oil company, and finally came to do what she really wanted to -- be a park ranger. The campsite is a virtual paradise of new trees and bushes planted everywhere as if it was the personal back yard of a rancher-turned-forester. As I hit the sleeping bag tonight I am leaving off my tent fly and watching thousands of stars twinkle above me.

June 5 (to Independence point; Lake Sakakawea)

Enjoying the Lewis and Clark State park so much I hung around a few hours seeking the least excuse of a cloudy sky or heavy wind to force a second night here, but alas, the sky is blue and the water is glass. So I packed up.

Just at the southern turn into Big Bend is the village of New Town. Across the bridge on the right side is 4 Bears Casino. Parking my canoe I climbed the hill and wandered through the casino watching the zombie-like customers sitting at rows of machines, peep-hole-like, dropping coins down its throat as if they were in a trance. When someone won, there was little excitement, they just used the bucket of winnings to pump more coins back into the machines as if they were required to stay until their money ran out.

I ate a hamburger, and watched them set up for a gigantic outdoor rock concert that night. Listening to the sound check pretty well helped me decide not to stay at the adjacent campground, so I returned to my canoe and shoved off again.

Canoeing down around the curve of Big Bend I was headed toward Pouch Point when I discovered ahead of me a life-vest clothed lad in the water beside his Wave Runner. It was his first time out and he had fallen off and couldn't remount the thing. I tried to help, but the lad was so fat, even with my help he couldn't get back on. I tried to talk him into leaving the Wave Runner and letting me pull him into the bay. His response: My dad would kill me." So I hooked up to the wave runner, with the Buddha-like lad clinging to the back of it, and began towing the whole lot to Pouch Point.

A mile later my motor overheated and shut down. Now, here I am, still a half-mile from shore, with a dead motor, an overloaded canoe, a dead Wave runner, and a fat kid chattering in the water, and still no other boats in sight.

The next half mile was the longest half-mile paddle I've ever done.

At the shore he was met by his father, sure enough. Glancing disdainfully at the whale-like kid he muttered, "idiot," went and started up the wave runner... and immediately roared off on his own to make sure it was OK. The soaking wet boy, on the other hand gave me a soaking wet hug me and said, "Thanks! I hope your motor will be OK." Waiting a half hour for it to cool down, it did start again, and I crossed the bay to a delightful gravel beach on Independence Point where there are coyote tracks near my tent site tonight.

June 6 (at Independence point -- storm bound)

Awoke this morning in a thunderstorm, smiling at my opportunity to stay late. Smiling that is, until lightning stuck the trees in the little crescent of cottonwoods behind me, crashing louder than the rock concert sound check.

I crawled deeper in my sleeping bag and covered my head, as if that gave me more protection. Watching what a thunderstorm can do to one of these lakes has convinced me to never be caught in one while on the lake. Snuggled in my cozy tent I brewed some spice tea from a few tea bags from the Ft. Peck Hotel. I'm drinking "Reincarnation Spice Tea." The label says, "In a past life, perhaps you spent an evening in Marco Polo's camp on a return trip from the spice markets of the far east." Yeah, sure.

The lake has stirred up -- not just to rollers -- but to outright breakers, white-capping all over the lake from a steady north wind. Today will be a stormbound day -- that's fine, it is Sunday and I need a day for worship, rest, reading and writing.

After a steady downpour all morning I took a long leisurely nap -- after all, perhaps the storms of life are designed to cause one to slow down, think back and take a rest.

Awakening in early afternoon to bright sunshine and gradually diminishing waves I decided to overhaul my little kicker. Never comfortable with internal combustion engines, the little Johnson booklet gave me adequate instructions, so I changed the gear case oil and put in a new spark plug and fuel filter. On a test drive it ran at least as good, and it seemed to me a little better.

June 7 (to Garrison Dam)
The dawn came with clear skies and a heavy northern tailwind so I put in the lake at five AM and roared to Garrison Dam, discovering I could combine "tacking" with "surfing" and let the wind do lots of the work for me.

I landed at Sakakawea State Park I met a delightful college student and summer staff ranger, Brandy DuLoit, who cheerfully offered to close down her office and portage me across the dam on her lunch break.

After a short hop to the Downstream Campsite I set up camp yearning for a hot shower but first thinking of my mail drop at the nearby Riverdale. Asking directions for the 4 mile walk into Riverdale, campground hosts Chuck and Nancy Proper would hear nothing of it, and took me first to Riverdale to pick up my mail, then across to the other side of the dam (and a different time zone) to Pick City for grocery re-supply.

Chuck is a retired UPS driver from Lansing Michigan, who with Nancy has no permanent home, other than their trailer in which they live as campground hosts all around the US. Interested in river trekking themselves, they invited me to their trailer for home made Pizza and MYO salads that evening. Wonderful! The only drawback of the entire evening was the delicious coffee of which I drank too much, laying awake past two AM before finally dozing off.

June 8 (to Washburn ND plus some)
A frustrating day. Got off early with secret thoughts of making it all the way to Bismarck, but was quickly slowed down by the many sandbars and shallows below the dam which come up surprisingly in the very middle of the half-mile wide river. (Eventually I learned that the middle of the river is the most likely spot for sand bars, and the ten feet right next to the shore is often the most reliable deeper channel) At one point I became stranded in three inches of water and finally got out and walked the canoe through the river, Lewis-and-Clark style for

several hundred yards in the bitter cold water. (The water is always coldest below the dams. The dam intake is often 80-90 feet deep, thus letting out the coldest of the lake waters.)

On breaking a shear pin from hitting a hidden boulder I paddled to shore to discover all five shear pins in my case are fatter than the hole. This led to an hour of playing "metal lathe," filing a one inch long shear pin until it was smaller in diameter.

On the river again I made several miles before hitting a submerged log and shearing my new finely honed pin. Not willing to file another down I saw an abandoned fence on the shore, paddled over and used a piece barbed wire for a temporary shear pin.

That got me to the Washburn Bridge where the local Rural Water Manager took me to town in his pickup and I purchased several "rolled pins" which might get me to Bismarck where I am told there are several marine outlets. I usually plan for all kinds of cushions in gear, but I've sheared more then 10 pins in the last 1000 miles. I underestimated how many I'd need.

After ten more downstream miles, and threatening storm clouds rolling in, I figured I was half way to Bismarck and I set up camp on a gravel ledge in early afternoon, falling immediately to sleep as soon as I set up the tent, making up for the coffee-sleep on the night before. I figure it is about 40 river miles (26 line of sight-GPS miles) to Bismarck.

The two redeeming features of this day: (1) I came upon a white tail deer swimming across the Missouri today. Slowing down to keep pace I followed it over within a few yards (hastening its pace I suspect) amazed at the full half-mile swim. And, (2) a large bag of Doritos and cheese dip for lunch.

June 9 (to Bismarck ND)
I arrived in Bismarck by noon anticipating my wife's arrival by plane the following day, taking out at the city landing site. I called Enterprise car rentals and met Brian Winczewski over the phone who took me on as a personal project. Completely out of cars, Brian promised to figure something out. I spent the next few hours sorting all my gear, dividing what would go home with my wife who was bringing my summer gear .

With no cars showing up, Brian eventually took the afternoon off, brought a pickup truck to the river and loaded in all my gear, then offered to store the canoe over the weekend inside the Enterprise garage -- amazing second-mile service! Eventually I was sent away in a 15 passenger van for the night, until a smaller car was turned in.

After wandering the shopping mall wide-eyed at all the devices, the colors, and the smells, I spent the night in the moderately-priced-moderately-satisfactory Expressway Inn. As always when trekking, I had a poor night's motel sleep. Used to lapping water, the sounds of nature, and even thunder and raindrops on my tent fly, my sleep was constantly disturbed by every slamming door, toilet flushing upstairs, or truck passing by outside -- all unusual sounds to my mind now.

June 10-13 (at Bismarck ND R&R)
Celebrating our 32nd. anniversary, and the 1000 mark of my trek, my wife, Sharon arrived by air and we spent a delightful weekend in North Dakota and Montana, retracing some of the sites on the trek thus far, and visiting the Lewis and Clark sites I missed from the river.

June 14 (to Ft. Yates ND)
True to form, Brian from Enterprise trucked my canoe back to the river and Sharon stayed to see me off. Most trekkers take R&R days with loved ones after a month or two -- but they always leave the trekker feeling more lonesome afterward. I sure am. Sharon saw me off from the shore and waited until I was out of sight. Canoeing through the rest of Bismarck I kept hoping she'd drive around to the southern end of town and I'd get to see her once more. But I never saw her, and left town feeling more lonely than when I arrived. (I later discovered that she *did* drive to the southern end of town, and hid out of sight to watch me disappear again, thinking that if I had actually seen her, I might have given up on this whole idea of a river trek and gone home with her!)

I decided to put in a 12 hour day pushing all the way to Ft. Yates. I hitched a ride to the gas station in the back of a truck driven by an Indian woman. (I had updated my terminology to "Native American" several years before, but consistently in my interaction with "native Americans" they referred to themselves as "Indians.")

In the back of this truck I rode with a five year old and a three year old, who bounced around with me as the woman drove faster that I thought one might drive with pre-schoolers in the back. But the children knew how to cling top the side rails and I too copied their style. Returning to the canoe I went down river another ten miles to Langeliers Bay, a L&C site, popping up my tent as the sun started to hide behind large ominous clouds. Too tired to cook I opened a can of Swanson chicken and made a sandwich. I'm 77 miles downstream from Bismarck, perhaps the maximum miles possible on lake water. Now to bed.

June 15 (to Mobridge SD)
An exceedingly slow start... first paying down the debt from yesterday's long day. I kept finding little things which needed done and didn't get off until 10:30, four hours after waking. I met the Klosterman family -- Ben Klosterman and his dad and cousin who arrived about ten to launch their boat. They are on a one-week Missouri river fishing trip though they practically live on the Mississippi in Minnesota. Ben, an obviously motivated twelvish lad took my photo, then proceeded to interview me, taking careful notes on a little piece of paper. That boy will make something of himself. The trick is to find what lights a boy's fire -- then feed it fuel. Here must be a future journalist.

Canoeing down to Mobridge in a steady downpour, interspersed with heavy drenching, I was rewarded by a Burger King right on the water! After an adequate input of Burger-fat, and using the telephone to send and receive my e-mail messages, I walked to the grocery store, then met a sweet lady in the fishing tackle store who gave me the lowdown on camping below Mobridge.

Back on the water, (actually *in* the water, for the rain is pouring now) I added the few miles to get to Indian Creek Rec. Area where I found fuel at the marina and pulled out on a sandy beach and am sharing a campsite with a fishing couple from North Dakota.

Today was one of those days when one wonders why I am doing this. It is difficult for others to understand, but after a month of trekking, the opposition is no longer sleeping on the ground, lack of a shower, or even a steady rainstorm... it is quite simply: boredom. Same sights, mile after mile. If I were plopped down here directly from "regular life" it would be awe inspiring. But after a month of it, this is now "normal" and like anything impressive it eventually gains an insipid sameness if seen day after day.
However, I know that these feeling often pass after a few days or weeks, and something new to see shows up. So I plod on.

June 16 (to Forgot-the-name Bay)
A nice calm day following the rain of yesterday (and most of the night). A slight breeze pushed me along to a morning break at a small bay where I met Jim and Serene Vance, out fishing

from Great Falls Montana. I discovered that they had been taught canoeing by Jim and Diane McDermond, the Medicine River Canoe people who had portaged me around Great Falls. Serene slipped over to the pit toilet and walked up to a rattlesnake which promptly disappeared into a hole near the base of the outhouse. Gee, thanks! My dad once told me a story of a fellow who got snake-bit in the rump at a pit toilet and I've never sat on one since without imagining the possibility... now I have another reason to think of that remote possibility! I decided to move on.

Stopping at West Whitlock bay for an ice cream bar and phone call I then floated on down the river to a forgot-the-name bay where a South Dakota fish warden was posted to check out the take of fishermen getting out at the site. My fee for the campsite was to listen to a few hours of typical "Dakota griping" before the warden finally called it a day and left me alone with the meadowlarks and barn swallows on this quiet bay. He was the sort of fellow who would call into to daytime radio shows to gripe about unseen powers or were out to rip everybody off. "The game is all rigged" was his most common expression." He finally left me. And left me with a throbbing headache.

Setting up my tent, the last of the day's fishermen came in, two retired couples. In conversations they were so fascinated with the trek that they unloaded fresh carrots, two apples, several bunches of grapes and ice cold Cokes in my lap as their contribution to the trek.

Grateful, I gobbled it all down immediately, took a bath in the river, read an hour and went to bed, somewhat rejuvenated.

June 17 (to Ft. Sully Game Refuge--big bend)
I woke up this morning to a stiff southeast wind, a bad sign. I am headed Southeast from now on. I broke camp and once I got out of the bay -- Wow! The wind was white-capping the waves and I faced higher and higher waves. I was soaked by every breaker crashing over the bow (or often gunwale) of my canoe. My hidden goal had been to make it all the way to the dam today... but after going around the corner of the Ft. Sully big bend the wind hit me straight on and the waves turned to three foot high surf - which means when I am in the trough the tops of the waves beside me are about shoulder level. I continued climbing the waves, pausing on the top a while, then slamming down into the trough plowing the bow into the next wave... until one particularly giant wave tossed me forward at such a speed that the bow completely disappeared under the next wave. Though the reliable canoe bounced back out (thanks to the snapped-on cover) I had had enough and headed for a crescent of gravel beach just around the big bend corner.

Still early, I pitched my tent to read and wait out the wind. Glad for my small library at times like these! But all afternoon the waves crashed on shore, until I eventually had to pull my boat out another several feet to keep the rising waves from swamping it even with the cover tightly snapped down. Finally I gave up -- I will spend the night here.

June 18 (to Brule Big bend, Lake Sharp, SD)
Raining intermittently all night, often accompanied with thunder and lightning, I awoke not expecting much. And I got what I expected -- three foot waves breaking so that the water looked like white frosting on a cake.

About ready to stay another day, I began figuring when I'd arrive in Lower Brule for my mail drop and realized if I wasted another day here I'd have to wait over Sunday in Lower Brule, for the post office to open. Examining the waves again, the new information seemed to make them shrink. So I stuffed all my gear into my 15' canoe and took off in larger waves and stronger wind than I probably would have under normal situations.

Slamming from wave to wave, climbing up one to slam down into another, with every wave breaking over the bow soaking me full in the face, I hammered through the storm for half a day before the waves finally dropped to 2' and I only had to bail out the canoe once every 15 minutes (instead of every five minutes).

By afternoon the waves had calmed to ordinary and I arrived at Oahe dam, happy to bid this endless two-state lake good riddance. At the dam I met another Dakota Game, fish and Parks "fish warden" who was at a loss to know how to help me around the dam. But, the first "fisherman" I asked happened to be a research supervisor in the fisheries department who ordered the don't-know-how-warden to call the office and "get some help for this guy." The warden dialed the number then handed me the phone, "Here you talk," he said. (Dakota fish wardens are a curious lot).

However, John Lott, the Senior Wildlife Biologist happened to answer the phone and said, "Sure, I'll be over myself in a few minutes to help you." John showed up in ten minutes with his truck and happily hauled me around the dam. Total time from landing to launching: one hour. I camped at the upstream end of the Brule Big Bend (there are lots of "big bends" on the Missouri).

June 19 (to Chamberlain SD)
Wanting to get as close to Lower Brule as possible, figuring the Post Office would only be open to noon on Saturday, I pushed right to nine o'clock last night down Lake Sharpe, and camped right before the Brule Big Bend. The site I selected, however, turned out to be a favorite party spot for the town's local teens, who determined to celebrate "It's Friiiiiiiiday!" with an all-nighter, just 50 yards from my tent. Taking a Crocodile Dundee attitude ('Jes kids having fun") I stuffed in a set of ear plugs and slept reasonably well. At 5:30 AM they were still going strong, which was time to rise anyway. The "Big Bend" makes almost a full loop, coming back to the 1 1/2 mile neck after circling 25 miles. So I am only a few miles from the post office now -- but have about 25 miles of river to get there.

The problem: fog. this morning's fog is so thick I could not see beyond 50'. Bent on getting my mail, and not wanting to do the road walk, I discovered the real value of my GPS receiver. On the map I calculated points around the bend and entered them in my GPS. Then I "flew blind" the next 25 miles, only seeing the looming shoreline three times in the entire morning.

Amazingly I arrived in Lower Brule just fine! I walked into town asking about the Post office and was told "the postmaster usually comes in by 10:00 or 10:30, but catch her quick -- she leaves before 12:00. Ordering a breakfast at the ever-present casino, I waited until 10:30 and returned to the PO tapping on the metal door after hearing rustling inside. A woman's voice called out, "Come back at 11:15." I cheerfully said, "sure," to which the governmental voice replied, but don't come after 11:45, I'll be closed then." Well, that gave me a precise window at least.

Sure enough, the window opened at 11:15 and I collected my cards, notes, letters (even home-baked cookies from Sharon) and walked back to my canoe in the "park."

A short hop downstream and I came to the Big Bend dam and saw a fellow sort of waiting around with his boat on his trailer. Denny Lee, from Zumbrota Minnesota was waiting for his family to meet him with bait. He cheerfully offered to take me around Big Bend dam and into Lake Francis Case. Elapsed time: 30 minutes. These people are wonderful.

I purposed to make it to Cedar Shore Resorts on the right bank at Chamberlain SD. I had stayed in the campground on my way out to Three Forks and said to myself, "If I make it down this far I'll stay in the *hotel* next time." And the nice twist is this: Tomorrow is father's day so I will celebrate two things: Father's day and the fact that on this very day I crossed the 1000 mile countdown line -- from Chamberlain it is "only" 969 miles to St. Louis. Sally, at the marina ,remembered me from my night well over a month ago, and with a few strings pulled, I had myself a huge room at a special canoe trekker's price.

June 20 (to Oahe Dam)

Though wanting to delay my exit from the comfy resort as long as possible, I dared not, for now I was set on one thing: Sioux City, Iowa and a week's break was stored up for me before I made the final push to St. Louis. I headed out into a brisk south wind which quickly stirred up into a ferocious sea. Slamming from one wave to another trying to unseat me from my bucking bronco canoe. Since my wife might read this journal I won't even describe the height of this day's waves, suffice it to say that from the trough I had to look *up* to see their tops.

Complicating my dilemma was a leaky canoe. The constant slamming of the last few weeks apparently loosened some of the rivets in the usually sea-worthy Grumman craft. I now get ankle-deep water in the canoe every 10 minutes, which works OK in calm seas, but is complicated to pump out while trying to maneuver the canoe across the waves. On a calm sea a leak is minor. On these South Dakota storm-driven angry waves it is a threat and demoralizing. I am wanting to be done with the lakes... indeed the entire trek! I know all about "middle miles malaise" which trekkers experience... but that does not make the malady any less fierce when one gets infected.

My over-riding goal of this week is to get to Yankton SD and the Gavin's Point Dam , the last of these wind-cursed lakes. I need a bigger boat or smaller water! Not able to trade the boat... I will be delighted to trade the wide open lakes in for a mile-wide river. What a relief it will be.

There is nothing else of import to report for this day. I saw no beautiful sites, enjoyed no majestic wildlife, drank in no views -- only drinking the ice cold lake water smashing into my face as my boat climbed the giant rollers, then nose-dived into the next trough, the bow piercing the base of the wave as water broke over the top of the canoe into my face. Then I repeated it again. And again. And again all day. I am not proud of going out today. But I am driven to get to Sioux City and my "malaise break" thus I am willing to canoe from 5:30 AM to 9:30 PM in higher-than-I-should-have seas. I got to the dam at dark and collapsed into bed too worn out and sore to cook supper so I ate a dry bagel, too weary to spread it with peanut butter.

June 21 (to Sioux City, Iowa)
Up before the faintest trace of dawn believing I would indeed make Sioux City today no matter what. I ran full speed down river with the fast current released from the lakes until afternoon, arriving at Midland Marine in downtown Sioux

City. There is nothing else to report for this day. I saw only a blur of shoreline as I was driven to get to Sioux City, believing that my week off would rejuvenate my spirits and bring back the spice and excitement which the "middle miles" had drained from me.

Joel, the service manager at Midland Marine examined my canoe's leaks, discovering that it was more than rivets -- the actual aluminum was being torn and cracked from the constant slamming by the waves. Joel loaned some sandpaper to me and instructed me on making a (temporary) patch with special marine epoxy. He offered to let me store the canoe there until I return from my "vacation-from-vacation," as he called it. As the day closed out, I quickly patched my canoe, rushed to the airport, rented a car, and headed home to Indiana and Chicago where my son, John was flying in from a couple of months wandering around Europe -- I wanted to meet him at the airport and hear his fresh first report.

June 22 -- June 27
(Debriefing with son John and "Middle Miles Malaise" Break)

June 28 (To Omaha - Dodge Marina)
How refreshed I am from my week off! I am again drinking in the sites, watching the shoreline for game, smiling to myself as I float down this fast-flowing river. The break gave me the "Second Wind" I needed to finish the final leg of this trek.

Having received up to six inches of rain over the weekend in this area, the river is high and flowing as fast as 7 MPH according to my GPS receiver. If I can stay in the current it sweeps me down river at a rate of 50-60 miles a day before I add any on top of that.

I marina-hopped all day, collecting data for the guidebook and munching on snacks, eventually finding myself 110 miles downstream at Omaha Nebraska by early evening.

At the Dodge Marina I met the collection of old guys who gather each night at the docks to spin yarns and was fascinated to hear Bob Coleman talk of the yesteryears on the river. He gave me a copy of his book of yarns from the steamboat era which I planned to read before going to sleep.

On advice of Bob Coleman I went to the trailer of the Dodge Marina Manager to ask if I could camp there, but nobody answered the door. After a half hour wait I figured I'd slip outside the fence and set up my tent and read Bob Coleman's book.

It was not to be. Opening my food pack I discovered my "Honey bear" had burst open spreading honey over all my food, stove, and cooking utensils. Before reading the book I had to clean each item in the river, and I still feel sticky all over.

Just as I was about to settle in with Bob Coleman's book, the Marina manager showed up in his pickup truck to tell me to transfer my boat to the marina dock, and my tent to the grass in front of his trailer. Helping me along, we loaded the still-pitched tent in his truck, and I paddled my canoe back inside the gated marina and parked it at a dock designed for gigantic yacht-type vessels.

By the time I fixed my Lipton rice dinner, it was dark and I was only able to read one chapter of Bob's book before falling to sleep.

June 29 (To Brownville NE)
I was up and off under threatening skies to discover Bob Coleman, the book-writer waiting for me at the entrance to the cove for a final lingering visit. Bob had a stroke and a heart attack and is fearful he will never get to trek the Missouri, his life-long dream. His attitude was, "If you are going to die anyway, why not die on the river?" His family may not see it the same way. He does have a point, however.

Sure enough, a steady rain began in a half hour and drenched everything incessantly all day. I stopped at various closed-in-the-morning marinas and determined to buy one of those cheap breakfasts at the upcoming riverboat casino. But upon tying up near the jammed-at-eight AM parking lot, and finding the breakfast buffet, I gave up when I discovered half of Omaha had the same idea -- the line was 50 people long.

The river is at now flood stage, jammed full of logs, trees, and every other piece of junk imaginable from water heaters to plastic chairs, all floating downstream at about seven miles per hour. It is like riding a toboggan down through a forest of trees, only the trees are floating too. The river has overflowed its banks and flooded the adjacent fields, making finding a camping spot almost impossible.

At Plattsmouth Marina, the marina building itself was in the middle of the water, some 100' from shore, and thus closed. With the Platte adding to the flow (and flotsam) the river is now a tangled mess of trees, snags, and logs, with barely enough space between to maneuver a canoe. The real threat is to my little Johnson kicker -- which keeps slamming into underwater logs, breaking a shear pin, or in one case bending the motor keel.

So weary from dodging logs in the downpour, I basically missed Nebraska City and, yet was happy to be moving so fast, making it all the way to Brownville, Nebraska. The fast water has give me 100 miles per day average since Sioux City, even with time out for shear pin replacements, and I could "open it up" and do much better... and perhaps I will when I get closer to St. Louis.

At Brownville the park was completely flooded, so I canoed through the trees to the main road, and set up my tent on the shoulder, just two feet above the water. The owner of a "steamboat tour boat" was there who directed me to Midge's "Brownville House" for dinner and I ate an excellent rib eye steak, wonderful home-made bread, and followed it up with a regretful piece of pie. Returning to my tent down by the river I turned in at nine.

June 30 (To Atchison)
All night cars kept pulling in beside my tent to flash their lights on the rising river -- apparently river-watching is the all-night sport in Brownville. The parked cars didn't stay long enough for any other endeavor. Each time I was awakened I thought I ought to check the water level myself, just two feet below tent, but I figured if the water was getting close to my tent door certainly one of these drivers would tell me, so I'd roll over and go back to sleep until the next checker arrived.

At six in the morning I returned to the Brownville House to wash up and eat a two dollar breakfast. I ate it with Midge herself, the owner of the restaurant, who was not on duty last night when her son was managing the place. Staying there until eight catching up on my notes and writing, I was the only customer in that two hour period.

Returning to the river, I packed up my tent, and waded out to my canoe, now several hundred feet out in the water, tied to a tree, and headed downstream among the logs, trees, and other flood debris.

Continuing downstream I began calculating... having made two 100 mile days with relative ease, and figuring the remaining 535 miles... and fixed my eyes on the 4th of July... I decided to make 100 miles my minimum in this 7-8 MPH flood current.

Whizzing down river only to stop for quick walkabouts for the guidebook in Rulo and St. Joseph, I went into auto-drive mode in the steady downpour, winding up at Atchison right at dark, even more determined to get an earlier start tomorrow, but logging 112 miles just the same today. In the downpour I walked up the hill to the Comfort Inn for a dry night and calculated that if I could stay in the current for 15 hours, and open up my kicker to full speed, I might make more than 150 or miles a day, enough to get me to St. Louis by July 4.

July 1 (to Miami Bend)
Leaving the hotel before dawn I started back into the water just before the sky started to light up and stopped in Leavenworth (a depressing town) for breakfast, then straight through Kansas City, except for a stop at the Flamingo Casino to send e-mail (which didn't work anyway.) Then to Lexington to pick up my mail, including home baked cookies from Sharon, several packages of dehydrated fruit from Ed and Gervais Baptist of Richmond Virginia, Appalachian Trail companions from years ago, and a letter from a grade school student in Maine who is studying Lewis and Clark.

Regretting leaving Lexington, and tempted to stay at the boat ramp, I resisted the urge and returned to the water to eat up more miles,, before camping on a slice of dry levee land on the bend just before Miami Missouri, 263 miles from St. Louis, for a total of almost 160 miles in 15 hours. Superb! I can taste the finish line now, and it is a hard discipline to record notes for the guide -- I want to finish this trek on July 4 and go home and see my family and friends!

July 2 (To Hermann MO)
Tasting St. Louis strong now, I rushed down the flood tide at 15-16 MPH stopping only to do several quick walkabouts of the shore towns for the guidebook data. By evening I rolled into Hermann, Missouri excited to be at the 98 mile marker, and knowing (assuming my water pump holds out for another 100 miles of silt) that I could make it to the arch tomorrow.

What a neat town, right on the water! I arranged for a room in the B&B right on the river, a 100 year old rambling mansion decorated with antique furniture. The only drawback was the Amtrak train which shook the whole house periodically like a tornado, and Mary's cat which had apparently deposited its dander here and there enough to cause my outdoor-acclimated lungs to wheeze within 10 minutes.

I walked to town, called home, took one last breath of non-feline air and returned to my room for what could probably be my last night on the river.

July 3 (to St. Louis)
Waking up through the night every time a train rumbled past I hopped out of bed with a slight wheeze at five and was in the river by 5:30 AM believing I could finish the trek today. Flying down the still-flooded river I made the

Mississippi-Missouri confluence and saluted the Lewis and Clark monument on the Illinois side before clipping down the last 15 miles to the arch, my mistake of the day.

St. Louis had a 4th of July fair going on, with rides set up everywhere in sight around the arch, and thousands of people milling around in their carnival clothes. I landed my boat on the small waterfront street by the arch perplexed at the thousands of people milling around eating cotton candy. As I began to step out of my boat near a little booth selling elephant ears, one of St. Louis' policemen swaggered over to say, "Sorry, back in the water you can't dock here." I explained how I had come 2500 miles from Three Forks Montana to this arch. His reply: "I don't care if you came from China, you can't park that boat anywhere along this shore -- get back in the water."

Disgusted, I grumbled something to myself and pushed off for the other side for the ever-present casino, tied up near the shore and caught a far-too-expensive taxi to the airport where I rented a car to return to Indiana.

Returning within an hour to find my boat and equipment still OK (I was surprised) I loaded up my trunk wishing I had ended my trek 15 miles back at the peaceful, private, remote confluence of the Missouri and Mississippi.

However, as I unloaded my gear from the canoe this final time, thousands of mental pictures flashed through my mind like a slide show, running at warp speed: The first night beside the edge of that tiny stream at Three Forks Montana, portaging around so Canyon Ferry Dam, campsites on the shore of giant lakes, large towns like Great Falls, Bismarck, Omaha, Kansas City, and tiny towns like Ft. Peck City or Brownville or Hermann, thousands of wildlife photos including that deer swimming across the river, so many misty mornings on the river, dozens of faces of the helpful people throughout the trip, big barges steaming upstream, beautifully clear starlit nights, cozy days wind bound in my tent on the big lakes... and hundreds more memories flashed by faster than one could narrate... and I began to chuckle aloud.

Of course this St. Louis cop wouldn't understand! He put in his time, went home and sat all evening in front of his satellite TV. He, like most of the carnival crowd jamming the streets around the arch, was fully satisfied with the ordinary life.

As I loaded the last of my gear into the rental car and turned my faithful but leaky canoe loose to float away down river (with a note telling whoever found it they could have it) I decided that this arch experience was after all a perfectly appropriate finish to my trek. The St. Louis cop and the crowd of carnival tourists represented the majority of "normal" people. Those who would never understand why a person would take such a trek. "Why do a thing like that?" "Sounds like lots of work to me" "Do you get paid to do this?" "Why sleep on the ground for all that time?" "Where do you go to the bathroom?" They are like the St. Louis cop and the wandering tourists. Such folk will never understand.

But others do. They understand the call of the wilderness. The yearning to make a trek or pilgrimage. They too have secretly dreamed of making a trek or pilgrimage. Some day. When the timing is right. It is to these folk that I dedicate this guidebook -- people who want more than cotton candy and elephant ears.

--Keith Drury
St. Louis Missouri   July 3, 1999

5

TREKKING DATA

A point by point guide to the Missouri River, re-supply points, portaging the dams, and other helpful route information.

> *** Note concerning Missouri mileage**.
> *This guide will occasionally list official miles from the mouth of the Missouri at the confluence with the Mississippi. However, don't take the mileage too seriously until the final 735 miles, and even then not too seriously.*
>
> *Steamboat owners established the first mileage and charged on a basis of 3000 miles from the Mississippi to Ft. Benton (as far upstream as the steamboats ever got). Since Three Forks is about 250 miles above Ft. Benton that would make your trek 3350 miles, if you did the whole river.*
>
> *However, in the 1880's government engineers made an official survey and established the distance from the Mississippi to Ft. Benton as 2274 miles (the steamboat owners grumbled that they cut off all the bends and too all the shortcuts and the steamboats still had to go 3000 miles but were only paid for 2274 miles. So, taking this official survey figure of 2274*

miles, and adding the 250 miles above Ft. Benton brings your trek mileage to a bit over 2500 miles.

But it isn't that easy. The final 735 miles of the river is now "channeled" by the Army Corps of Engineers, straightening out many loops and bends effectively cutting out about 200 miles of river route, that reduces your route back to about 2300 miles.

And, finally, to complicate matters more, there is no exact route through the large lakes. Will go straight down the middle of the lake (I hope not, at least if you expect any wind). Follow the shore? (truly follow the shoreline and your journey will be closer to 4000 miles, forget it.) Or, (most likely) travel from "point-to-point" through the lakes taking neither the most direct route no the shoreline route.

It is easy to see why postcards picturing the Missouri report the length as everything from 2300 miles up to 3100 miles. It all depends on which Missouri River route you follow. This guide uses the most conservative number: 2320 miles. You will certainly travel more, but you know at least you traveled this far.

THREE FORKS, MONTANA   Mile 2320
N 45.56   W 111.29

The small town of Three Forks Montana boasts a grocery store (with a grouchy check out lady) gas stations, bank, the Headwaters Cafe and for an overnight stay the Sacajawea Inn, a hundred year old traditional wood hotel.

The town of Three Forks, however is not exactly at the three forks The actual launch site is about four miles out of town across the four-lane highway at the Three Forks state park. The Jefferson and Madison streams join first, then the Gallatin joins in. At this point, there is a launch site on the left of the road just before leaving the park. The handout newspaper says camping is permitted at the launch site, but the fish and game people might try to tell you otherwise. Here the river is clear and fast moving, with rocky bottom. If you have rented a car you will most likely be returning it to Helena (which you will pass later on your trek). The hitch back from Helena is an easy one, though you may have to walk the 4 miles from the four-lane.

TOSTON DAM, MT
N 46-07.300   W 111.24.554
Your first dam, and an easy portage. This dam really doesn't make a lake per se, but merely raises the river level for a short way. The portage is on the left at the dock near the picnic shelter.   There are two put-ins, the shortcut put-in about half way down to the other boat launch, but you have to drop down a pretty steep bank. The dam boys say you should watch for rattle snakes around this dam. There is a nice campsite at long put-in at the base of the hill.

TOWNSEND, MT   2275 Right
Put in on the right bank just after both bridges and take the mile walk to center of town or

make the easy hitch. Townsend has gas, phone, groceries, and plenty of friendly folk to talk with.

CANYON FERRY LAKE, MT
If you are canoeing early in the season you may canoe through marshland quite a way into Canyon Ferry Lake. Later in the season when the lake has been filled from snow melt, the river ends quicker and the lake begins sooner. This is your first big lake, and though you may later dismiss it as small, right now it looks huge. Be careful, angry storms can blow up and produce waves as high as your canoe is long.

GOOSE BAY MARINA , MT
N 46-32.424   W 111.33.625
On the right bank of Canyon Ferry Lake on an inlet about 60% up the lake. A shabby private marina and campground hardly worth visiting unless you really need some cheap snacks or must use the telephone.

KIM'S MARINA, MT
N46-39-060   W111-42.017
A delightful quality marina and campground well worth a stop. Camping is about $10 but a shower is $2 (ask for a towel even though it normally is not provided). Gas, groceries, mail-drop, and across the street is O'Malley's Pub and restaurant where you'll want to try their "Cowboy Classic" and "Indian Fried Bread." And, if you have a motor and need help see "Butch's Marine" (in a garage behind

O'Malley's). Butch is one of those garage mechanics who can fix most anything even without consulting a computer.

CANYON FERRY DAM, MT
N46-39.378   W111.44.200

Get ready for a major painful portage. Portage right up a steep shale bank, across the road, over the concrete wall, and down a steep so-called "path" to the put-in site below the dam. Don't expect much help from the dam employees (who were right there with a pick up truck when I portaged and even wanted to help me portage, but when they called their supervisor were told to refuse help). Later, at a lower dam I was told by one of the employees that there is a federal law requiring them to provide assistance to portaging canoes, but I have been unable to locate the law. If there isn't a law their should be -- after all, *they* put the obstruction there, and the river is the highway!

If you are solo and have a heavy canoe this portage could take a full half-day. A much better idea than trying this worst-of-all-Missouri River Portages is to put in at the boat launch about a mile before the dam on the right, and find a fisherman with a boat trailer or pickup truck to take you around the dam.

HAUSER DAM, MT
Portage on the left up a bank to a gradually descending road. Some ignore the signs and go right up to the shore at the dam, but do so at the risk of a $500 fine (the fines are not levied by

Montana Power employees, but by the fish and game cops). The workers at Hauser Dam are much more trekker-friendly than those at Canyon Ferry and if you ask them they will likely toss your stuff on their truck and take you around the dam to the put-in site below the rapids. (Don't put in before the regular put in site -- this dam collapsed once and the iron from the old dam is strewn over the floor of the river waiting to tear out the bottom of your boat in this fast tail water.)

As you move toward the Gates of the Mountains be ready for a fast-flowing river which seems to sink away from you as if it is a long descending highway, yet without the usual "rapids" such a drop would normally give the canoeist. It is an exciting trip.

GATES OF THE MOUNTAINS BOAT CLUB N46-49.905 W111-57.115
A great place to stop for a break, especially if you precede the tourist season. From here the boat tours of the "Gates of the Mountains" begins and ends. This boat club is run by a trust fund of sorts, and they have some delightful displays in the "waiting shelter." Also several Coke machines and a phone.

COLTER CAMPSITE, MT
N46-51.563 W111-54.500
There are two (official) campsites right down in the "Gates" canyon. If at all possible try to plan your day to stay a night down in this canyon. The Colter Campsite is a canoe-in site,

and if you beat the season it will give you a delightful night in the canyon. (I had the entire site to myself, and had a wonderful stay.) Watch for the sign on the right... but it will be hard to miss -- after all you are in a canyon!

THE BOAT LOFT, MT
N46-59.330 W111-59.061
On the right bank just before Houlter Dam. A great place, staffed by friendly people, great snacks and groceries, (and free coffee) A wonderful service shop if you need motor repairs or shear pins. However, don't bother asking for a portage -- the very idea of a "Boat Loft" bans all boat trailers from the property.

HOULTER DAM, MT   2215 Miles 2215
N46-59.555 W112.00.549
Portage left where you can canoe right up to the dam. Take the long gradual road to put in site. There is a shortcut put-in down shale bank right at the cable limit signs, but having taken the short cut route I wish I had taken the longer walk. The river moves fast down through the next canyon... enjoy the speed, it won't last.

CASCADE, MT
N47-16.240 W111-41-765
Land under the bridge on either bank. Cascade has several gas stations, an IGA grocery store, a convenience store, phone, PO and more bars than it needs. The river widens and slows from Cascade to Great falls, sticks floating on the

surface barely move but the area is teeming with bird life.

ULM, MT
N47-25.052   W111-30.222
Land on either the left or right bank. It is four blocks left to the gas station (at the Interstate 15 exit) and next door is the PO, phone, and of course, there are several bars in the area.

GREAT FALLS, MT   2120 MILES
It took Lewis & Clark a full month to portage the Great Falls. You will do it faster, but it can be complicated. The Great Falls series drops 512' over several miles (for comparison Niagara Falls drops about 150'). An easy take out is just above second bridge on the left bank. Two blocks to the left on Central West Road is Great falls U-Haul-- Dick Ferrell, the manager came to Montana to study forestry and wound up running the U-Haul business. (Phone 406-761-1620) Hauling your canoe & gear around the series of falls in a U-haul truck then hitching back to your gear is one option. (about $60 with per-mile charges.)

A much better option is to contact Jim & Diane McDermond (406-761-0303) of the Medicine River Canoe club. Jim and Diane, along with other club members will portage thru-trekkers. Indeed, if you are going to get a portage from Jim and Diane, you will want to canoe closer to the first dam.

Great Falls is a good town for a day off. There are cheap motels near the fairgrounds/ U-haul. A better hotel a mile away toward K-mart (Day's Inn @ $42.) Right next to Day's Inn is Big Bear Outfitters which carries the stuff you forgot to buy for your trek.

The one-hour photo is at Wal-mart. But, while you are in Great Falls, don't miss a trip over to the Lewis & Clark Interpretive Center on the right bank. This is the best L&C site on the entire river. Also, Richard Hopkins the BLM field manager is helpful (downtown-ask for directions) where you can pick up the Tyvek maps for the Wild & Scenic River section coming up, if you want additional official maps.

Put-in sites below the dams: There are two. If you are comfortable with class two (and sometimes three) rapids, put in just below Merony dam (and stay mostly to the left the next three miles.) Otherwise go to Carter Ferry. Ask Jim and Diane for advice on this and also make sure you get Diane's advice on the White Cliffs sites -- she is a virtual fount of detailed and helpful information.

FT. BENTON, MT 2070 Miles
A delightful town which deserves an overnight stay. Don't miss the keelboat on main street. Everything you need is available here, a pleasant grocery store and fuel at the gas station a block or so north of the blinker light. While sometimes there is reliable safe water in the Wild and Scenic river, your best bet is to carry

water from here to last you until Kipp landing, 150 miles later.

WILD AND SCENIC RIVER/WHITE CLIFFS, MT

Probably the highlight of your entire trek. You will likely decide to return and do this section again, with your friends. On a trek one often does not stop to investigate enough, realizing that you've still got several thousand miles to go. This is a wonderful place to leisurely explore. In summer it is a very popular trip, so you won't be alone. Before May 31, however, you may be alone through this section, unless you are traveling through on a weekend.

Enjoy this segment of your trek, take your time, and be sure to walk up some of the trails -- the stories about rattlesnakes are overblown.

You will exit the Wild and Scenic River at Kipp campsite where you will find the only phone in the 300 mile section between Ft. Benton and Ft. Peck. As for groceries, your Benton groceries will have to last to Wolf Point, below Ft. Peck dam.

FORT PECK LAKE, MT

If you didn't get your sea-experience on Canyon Ferry Lake, here's your second chance. This 134 mile long lake is sometimes 5 miles wide and can kick up rollers as high as your boat is long. If it does you'll be wind bound. However, it is often peaceful and a canoeist can make it through the entire lake on glass. It depends on the wind. But a wise trekker will take enough food and water to allow for a day or two being storm-bound.

As to food, phone, and fresh water there is none in this full section. You must rely on the water you got at Kipp, and the food you got in Ft. Benton.

There are several official "campsites" on the shoreline, but these offer no services or water, but may offer companionship if you are lonesome, which you likely will be, considering you are trekking through more than 300 miles without so much as a store or town. Besides, if there are any fishermen who drove the 90 miles of dirt roads to get to the deserted shoreline, they often brought a cooler and Cokes along and will likely share one with you.

If you carry a GPS receiver it will no longer be a toy on this big lake where the dead-end arms are sometimes wider than the main channel. While most trekkers do not leave their GPS running all day, they do get it out when lost, plotting their location on their map so they can find their way back to the main channel.

FORT PECK DAM, MT 1770
Portage right if you insist on carrying everything yourself. If you are going to try to get a ride, portage at the marina on the left of dam and do one of three things: 1)ask someone off-loading their boat to portage you; 2) ask the guy at the marina to carry you around; 3) or, if you are staying at the Hotel (and you should)

call them for a portage (hey, Montanans are helpful people).

The put in site on the left bank is just below the outlet next to a nice campsite (with showers). The portage left is 4-5 miles if you have to carry it.

If you can afford a $32 night try the hotel "down town" (Pop 300). It was built in 1936 to house Corps of Engineers officers and has that substantial "New Deal flavor." Rooms have showers, but ask them to let you use the old claw foot bathtub upstairs - you'll need it by now. If you are a thru-trekker ask to use the hotel laundry. The hotel serves dinner in May "if enough people sign in." Later in the summer there is a reliable dinner. Their breakfast coffee is particularly delicious.

Find the Post office 200 yards from the hotel. The grocery store is no longer open so your Ft. Benton groceries have to last until Wolf Point. Unless, that is, you are willing to walk 4 miles out to the Conoco station to get a few snacks. If you do, look up "Sis Bondy" who volunteers in the little info booth. Sis, (Thelma is her real name) is in her 80's. She moved here before the dam was built in 1933 and is the oldest resident. She told me two hour's worth of stories not available in the official Corps releases. 30,000 people lived here then. Nearby is the original site of the fort. Oh yeah, across from the Conoco station see "The Gateway" and eat a 21 day aged New York Strip steak for $13. You'll like Ft. Peck. Have you ever seen the very first

LIFE magazine? That was this dam on the cover.

FT. PECK TO WOLF POINT, MT
This 62 mile section will be a big change from the giant lake. As always, after the dam the water is colder, the river is extremely shallow (depending on how much the dam boys are "retaining water" and the river is full of snags and boulders. The Indian reservation is on your left, and open grazing land to your right. While the run from Ft. Peck to the confluence is not as popular as the Wild and Scenic river, it is also both wild and scenic.

"Frazier rapids" can be class two (maybe three?) depending on water volume, but is not a difficult rapids. Oswego is near the river but hard to find access. Trees now are more common, and the rich bottom land will be lush with green grasses in early summer.

WOLF POINT, MT   1708
Unless the grocery store opens at Ft. Peck this will likely be your re-supply town for the run down to the Confluence and beyond. Wolf Point is a full service town complete with banks, grocery stores, hardware outdoor suppliers, gas and phone. Put in site is up a tiny inlet of Wolf Creek near the "pumping building" on your left. No dock or launch point.

It's interesting how towns have a collective personality, and the individuals of the town seem to take on that mind-set. In some towns if you walk a mile with a gas can, five cars will stop and offer you a ride. Wolf point seems to have an air of grim despair about it. I saw only one smile in my hour there -- and that was from a mildly retarded girl at the grocery store.

I made my purchases, walked the mile back to my canoe, paid $5 to the boys who had offered/threatened to watch my canoe for me, and got back on the river as quick as I could.

BROCKTON, MT 1649

Keep your eye out for the grain elevator on your left -- that's where you want to go. There are two ways to access this village: from the bridge (the long way) or take the left turnout and walk down the railroad tracks to the elevator.

Across from the elevator is the "B&S Quickstop" and gas station (including phone) which has an impressive array of food and snacks including a variety of tiny cans of meats. Just around the corner is the other business in town: "B&S laundry & Broasted chicken" (I am not making this up.) It really is a Laundromat/video store/broasted chicken combo store. If you need some deep fried chicken, get your fat fill-up here. The tiny post office has one of the friendliest postmasters on the route and is about the only thing in town not owned by B&S.

Even if you are not using Brockton as mail drop, stop in at the tiny Post office and talk with Bob. He'll get his map out and make you feel welcome to Brockton more than anyone.

FT UNION 1586
N 48-00 W 104-03

The signal to begin watching for the fort is floating under the black railroad draw bridge (once used as both a railroad and auto bridge, the automobiles having to make sure no train was coming before they zipped over the bridge). On your left is the reconstructed Ft. Union trading post. The river once flowed right past its front gate but has shifted its channel away leaving (in wet season) a marsh between you and the gate if you tie up in front of the fort.

Incredibly no attempt has been made to provide a dry path access to the fort directly from the river, and the general attitude from my interview with the employees as evidently "we don't want the hassle of boats landing." While this may be a typical attitude of many river sites, (i.e. "Millions for parking lots, but not one cent for river access") it was especially apparent at Ft. Union. With such an attitude pervasive, Randy Kane (head ranger) and Andy Bonta (site superintendent) may have been replaced by the time you arrive, and leadership with a more bicentennial trekker sensitivity may have their jobs. I hope so.

To tour the site without fording the swamp pass the fort until you come to highway 58 and put in on the left upstream from the bridge. Take highway 58 north a mile then turn left and walk down 1804 several miles to the fort.

THE CONFLUENCE   1584

Immediately following the fort is the Confluence of the Yellowstone and Missouri rivers. If you hit this section in late May or early June the Yellowstone will seem like the larger of the two rivers, having less "protection" by dams than the Missouri. If so, the Yellowstone will run muddy red, and you can actually canoe several hundred yards on the line, the left paddler canoeing in the Missouri, the right one in the Yellowstone.

The confluence is the most popular site for snaring paddlefish, those swordfish-looking creatures are seemingly leftover from another epoch. The fishermen cast a three-pronged snare far out into the river, then jerk it back hoping to snare one of these mothers-to-be on her journey upstream. They are giant fish, about the size of a child, and can weigh 150 pounds.

They are filled with little paddlefish eggs, sold for top dollar as caviar. If you arrive during the season (late May-early June) the shore may be lined with a hundred fishermen trying to snag one of these expectant mothers. A caviar company has set up shop here and has three or four full time men available to clean the paddlefish in exchange for the roe/caviar. There is a coke machine and water here during the season, but no supplies or phone, unless you arrive at the end of the season, then you may be able to talk some fuel out of the caviar company employees.

WILLISTON MARSH   1550

Be prepared for a tangled spaghetti bowl of channels, backwaters, oxbows and dead ends as you pass Williston. If you have excellent large scale maps and a GPS you will probably know where you are. Most trekkers simply keep going downstream assuming that all the channels will eventually reunite in the lake. They do, but be prepared for a winding tour of the marsh, first with the sun in your face, then on your right ear, then your back, and now in your face again!

If you didn't re-supply at Wolf Point, Poplar, or Brockton and you must go into Williston, there are two routes. The easiest (though longest) is to tie up at the bridge at US 85 and hitch 4-5 miles to US 2 then right 5-6 miles to Williston. The harder (and shorter walk) is to take the outer left hand loop which heads northeast to collect the Little Muddy River, then ascend the Little Muddy (assuming the water level is high enough) to the bridge carrying 1804 which is right in Williston. Neither are good access points, which is why Williston (like most larger cities) is not probably your best choice for re-supplying.

LAKE SAKAKAWEA

You'll love this long lake named for the wife of the Canadian trapped Toussaint Charboneau, Sakakawea (Hidatsa meaning Bird Woman). She was from the mountains above three forks, and had been captured and enslaved in a raid by the plains Indians, winding up the wife of a French Canadian trapper. She, along with her son on her back, accompanied Lewis and Clark and provided a vital link with the tribes where they hoped to get horses for their journey (a short one, they hoped) over the Bitterroot range of the rocky mountains and down the Columbia river to the sea. This lake (along with the new dollar coin) is in her honor.

The lake itself is 178 miles long and averages 2-3 miles wide, though it can get up to 5-6 miles wide occasionally. While "following the shore" is generally a good idea, the trekker has to cut off some points: the lake has 1300 miles of shoreline!

Consider the LEWIS AND CLARK STATE PARK, on the left shore (N48-06 W103-14) for a delightful walk-in/boat-in campsite right on the lake, yet with hot showers if you are needing one by now. This campground is tended by the ranger as if it is her personal garden and legacy -- you'll see more species of trees and bushes here than you've seen on your entire trip thus far.

Most trekkers stop at 4 BEARS CASINO (Mile 1481) (N47-59 W102-34.5) to eat a hamburger, make a phone call, or lose a quarter. They also have an adequate campground and gas station/quick stop. The landing for the campground and casino is past the bridge and casino around the corner to the bay on your right.

A much nicer public campground is located to the left, around the corner at NEW TOWN MARINA, a protected harbor and campground with showers, fuel, telephone and snacks.

Right at 4 bears you head south west as you round the big bend.

A substandard campground is located at POUCH POINT (N47-48 W102-24) around the corner to your left as you enter Van Hook Arm. (a better choice is the raw beach-inlet on the right bank at INDEPENDENCE POINT (N47.46.5 W102-21.3)

GARRISON DAM (RIVERDALE) 1391
This is a long portage, but you may be able to get help. Consider staying at Sakakawea State Park --Right on the point just before the dam. In the side office of the marina (fuel avail.) the state park ranger may be able to help you get around the dam, they sometimes portage canoe trekkers in their pickup truck.

If this fails, and there are no day fisherman putting in, the walk from the State Park is 2-3 miles. Some take out on the actual dam itself, near the intake building and walk up over the top -- this is probably the closest route to the put in site below the dam, but involves climbing the rip-rap.

Peck City on the right side of the dam has a small grocery store and gas station. Riverdale, on the left has a post office and snacks. The two towns are in different time zones.

The downstream campsite can be reached from the river. Look for a tiny sandy cove to your left with a metal pipe (draining a pond) emptying into it. Follow the path here 50 Yards to the campground. (Coke machine, showers, phone).

WASHBURN ND   1355

To your left after passing under the bridge is the landing. Follow this road up to Rt. 200 crossing the bridge then in to town. At the "gas station" on your right is an amazing hardware store. The town proper is behind the station. Across the street is an excellent Lewis & Clark interpretive center overlooking the river. At the time of the writing of this guidebook they had the actual original draft of the Thomas Jefferson letter of instructions to Lewis on display loaned to this center from the national archives. While all the interpretation is done well, you should especially study the 30' dugout canoe made from a cottonwood tree in the pattern used by Lewis and Clark. (Imagine portaging this around Great Falls, and you will readily see why it took a month!) The actual Ft. Mandan is three miles west of Washburn on county road 17, and the traditional site is 13 miles west.

This center offers an excellent bookstore and if you are running out of books to read on your journey it is a wonderful place to re-supply (see book list elsewhere in this guide).

BISMARCK/MANDAN   1315

If you started at Three Forks, congratulations, you have canoed over 1000 miles so far. However, don't relax too much yet -- you are not yet half way to St. Louis!

Bismarck is a large city and there are numerous take out sites., The first is the city launch site just past the "steamboat tour" on the left, after passing under the first bridge. There is a phone here. The second is at the large marina on your left a mile later. The final option is a launch site way down on S. Washington Street after you've apparently left town, but is still accessible to a private campground (up S. Washington street) and a few miles from the airport.

Bismarck has just about everything you need, though, as a large city it is difficult getting around it. If you need a rental car for taking a few days off to celebrate covering 1000 miles since Three Forks, I recommend Enterprise, with offices in the 100 block of Main Street, near the "steamboat" take out site. This company bent over backwards to help me in Bismarck, and you can count on "second mile service."

LAKE OAHE 1069
Soon after you leave Bismarck/Mandan the river starts to lose its flow and you begin to feel the effects of Lake Oahe. However, expect a multitude of trees, snags, and just-under-the-surface water-soaked logs for 20-30 miles.

The lake itself (pronounced O-wah-hee) is several miles wide, but has less bays and arms than either Sakakawea or Ft. Peck Lakes, making it very much like a three-mile-wide river. Of course the only current you'll sense is from the wind. Though Oahe is not as wide as those bigger lakes, it is pretty straight so if you've got a 15 mph wind coming down the lake, be prepared for waves and breakers.

FT. YATES

The boat ramp is before the town on your right, just to the left of the large grassy knoll. However, all the services are at the south end of town, so you might consider tying up another mile downstream (though, if the sea is choppy, the rocks will beat your canoe up if you plan to be gone long). Groceries, phone, PO, and fuel are about a mile from the boat ramp straight south through the residential area.

MOBRIDGE

A seemingly larger town then Ft. Yates with easier access. A full service town. You will be greeted at its edge by a large Burger King sign on the left bank, the first on-the-river BK in the last 1000 miles. And, if you started at Three Forks, you'll be willing to tie up on the suitcase sized rocks to have one!

South down the same street from the BK is a Payless full grocery store and just about anything else you want can be had in Mobridge.

If you can pass up the BK, but want a shower instead, pass to the Indian Creek Rec. Area and campsite/Marina. (second inlet on your left after town) However, if you want a sandy landing spot so your boat won't get beat apart on the rocks, take the third inlet and just around the corner is a sandy pull-out where you might be able to share the site with other campers. (N45-30.75 W100-22.75) The marina has short term supplies, cabins and fuel.

WHITLOCK BAY
On the left bank turn far back into the bay until you have almost made a circle to find Whitlock Bay ramp. Phone in the parking lot. North several hundred yards to the bait shop and snacks, drinks and ice cream. Campsite includes showers but few if any campsites on the water.

OAHE DAM 1069
Take out at right, a large landing site with plenty of fishermen happy to help canoe trekkers. If all fails, try calling the corps of engineers or Dakota game fish & parks at 605-773-5535. The put-in is below the dam at the marina which has a phone, snacks and fuel. If you need a major re-supply Pierre is just a few miles downstream on your left. Take out for Pierre is at the park on your left, hard to miss.

LAKE SHARP
Within a few miles of Pierre the river becomes Lake Sharp, some 80 miles long, constructed in 1963 between two Indian reservations, Crow Creek Sioux and Lower Brule Sioux. It is not much different than Oahe in feel.

THE BIG BEND
The dam you will portage later gets its name from the gigantic big bend in the river just before Lower Brule. Here the Missouri almost makes a complete loop, wandering 25 miles before returning the neck where you were quite a while ago, 1 1/2 miles across.

LOWER BRULE
Just after the Big Bend on your right. No landing site directly in town (though one above the town). The best take out site is at the playground on your right. Then walk through the campsite and South a few blocks to a tiny grocery store sometimes open, a hotel, Post Office, and casino. The only phone is in the casino (by the way, the best way to make money in a casino is to eat their inexpensive meals.)

BIG BEND DAM
Immediately following Lower Brule you will see the dam. Take out is at your far right all the way curled back around facing the generating plant (which looks like a spillway from the upper side). Like Oahe dam, this is also a busy site in fishing season, and if you ask right, you should be on the bottom side of the dam in an hour -- less on weekends. Ft. Thompson is a possible re-supply town, but if you can hold your horses for another 30 miles you can re-supply in Chamberlain.

CHAMBERLAIN 969
If you plan to overnight near Chamberlain, you have a left bank and a right bank choice. On your left is the town of Chamberlain. Take out at the American Creek Rec. Area (and campsite) or further up American creek in town itself). Chamberlain is a delightful almost-big-enough-for-a-movie town.

On the right bank is the Cedar Shore resort, including a restaurant, campground and marina (fuel). If you began in Three Forks, and are going to St. Louis, you might want to celebrate and get one of the rooms at the resort. If you do, request a "hillside room" (you've seen enough of the river recently) and ask for a special deal for canoe trekkers -- tell them where you started.

PICKSTOWN/ FORT RANDALL DAM 880
Take out on right at boat ramp near the dam. Put in on right below the dam and just above Randall Creek park campground.

If you plan to re-supply at Pickstown, on the other hand, take out is dam-left, up St. Francis bay and out is also on the left below the dam near the spillway campground. The spillway campground is close enough to walk to Pickstown, but the campground is less developed. (Though you can put in and camp on the right shore and canoe across.)

LEWIS AND CLARK LAKE
A short 25 mile lake, and your last one. Enjoy it, it is all river from here on.

YANKTON/GAVINS POINT DAM   806
(Lewis & Clark Lake)
Celebrate! This is your final dam portage! If you started at Three Forks, Montana you've portaged fourteen dams so far:

1. Toston Dam (river dam, MT)
2. Canyon Ferry Dam (Canyon Ferry Lake, MT)
3. Hauser Dam (River dam, MT)
4. Holter Dam (Holter Lake, MT)
5. Black Eagle Dam (Great Falls series, MT)

6. Rainbow Dam (Great Falls series, MT)
7. Cocharne Dam (Great Falls series, MT)
8. Ryan Dam (Great Falls series, MT)
9. Morony Dam (Great Falls series, MT)
10. Ft. Peck Dam (Ft. Peck Lake, Mt.)
11. Garrison Dam (Lake Sakakawea, ND)
12. Oahe Dam (endless Lake Oahe, SD)
13. Ft. Randall Dam (Lake Francis Case, SD)
14. Gavins Point Dam (Lewis and Clark Lake, SD)

You will not be saddened to bid the dams goodbye.   Take out for Gavins Point Dam is left of dam at the Lewis and Clark Marina. Put in is on the right near the Nebraska Tail waters campground.

SIOUX CITY 733 Left
A full size town with easy access from the river. Several pull-out sites, but one of the best is probably just below the "steamboat Visitor Center" on your left, at Midland Marina. Be sure to tour the free museum in the steamboat, "Sergeant Floyd," named for the single loss of life on the Lewis and Clark trek.

Passing through Sioux falls the Washington-Monument-type obelisk to you left is the 100 foot high Sergeant Floyd monument, who probably died of a ruptured appendix on the Lewis and Clark expedition. The only way for a river traveler to reach it, however is to dodge the traffic in I 29.

THE LOWER RIVER

From Sioux City to St. Louis you experience the third type of river: channeled "industrial canal." Here you will sail with heavy barges along a route the Corps of Engineers has established for barge traffic, not you. The navigation markers are frequent (red on the left, green on the right) and each one displays a mile marker showing the distance to St. Louis (actually to confluence of the Missouri and Mississippi, but until the day you arrive there you'll consider that close enough).

Besides the red and green markers setting out the left and right side of the channel, there are blue markers for many whole mile points, usually attached to a tree on the shore. Be ready to cross frequent "wing dams" or "wing dikes," (underwater stone dams to divert the flow into the channel). You'll drop a bit when crossing a wing dike, sometimes a bit more than "a bit" but nothing like the big waves you faced on the stormy lakes.

The lower river (especially when the flow is high) has plenty of full size "boils," with the water erupting like a volcano flowing outward. Canoeing into a boil makes it seem like an invisible underwater hand has grabbed your canoe and turned it, or is holding it back. The channel is pretty straight (the Corps of Engineer's constant "fixing" of the river has taken out more than 200 miles of river bends since Lewis and Clark).

The only difficult water you will face comes from the wake of the large barges. An upstream barge can cause two foot waves if you get close enough, and because of the narrow channel, the from-shore feedback waves last for nearly a mile after the barge has past you. If barge traffic is sparse, many canoeists simply take a "coffee break" and wait out the big waves. If traffic is heavier, you simply slow down and negotiate the wake and feedback. It is not as difficult as you have already faced on the big lakes.

MILE MARKERS From Sioux City
downstream the Corps of Engineers has posted frequent mile markers displaying the distance to the mouth of the Missouri at the Mississippi providing accurate locating of all sites from this point on. And by Sioux City the canoe trekker is "thinking St. Louis" it fits in with the "down to the finish line" mind-set. The mile markers for the major points from here on:
733 L - Sioux City
691 L - Decatur Marina
651 R - Cottonwood Marina
627 R - Dodge Marina
617 R - Sandpiper Marina/Omaha
601 R - Bellevue Marina
591 R - Plattsmouth
561 R - Nebraska City Bridge
535 R - Brownville
498 R - Rulo
449 R - St. Joseph
423 R - Atchison
397 R - Leavenworth
365 R - Kansas City
317 R - Lexington
262 R - Miami

```
226 - Glasgow
197 - Boonville
144 - Jefferson City
105 - Gasconade
 98 - Hermann
 67 - Washington
 44 - Rt 40 bridge
  8 - Rt. 67 Bridge
  0 - Mississippi River
+15   to St. Louis Arch
```

DECATUR MARINA Mile 691 RIGHT
Bob Hutton sold off his pizza franchises and downsized his life a few years ago opening this well-protected small marina in a little cove on your right Fuel and a few snacks available through the day, and full delicious meals in the evenings at his Pop N' Doc's Restaurant. No public phone, but ask Bob to use their marina phone if you are making a toll-free call.

HUFF ACCESS 680.3 LEFT
A delightful small campground with a hand pump, 20 campsites, and a shelter. Nothing more, but a nice private place.

LITTLE SIOUX CAMPSITE 669 LEFT
A full service RV-type campground.

COTTONWOOD MARINA 654.4 RIGHT
New owners are refurbishing this marina. Public phone, evening meals on weekends, and bar snacks. A protected cove to right, but public landing right on the river.

BLAIR 148.5 RIGHT
The landing site is just before the railroad bridge on your right at a little park. Potential re-supply by walking the mile into Blair.

NEW CAMPGROUND   640.6 LEFT
On your left, a new well-designed campground.

DODGE PARK MARINA   627.4 LEFT
A massive (expensive) marina for massive (expensive) boats. Here you'll see boats from St. Louis and suddenly you'll feel like you are on the final leg of your journey. Fuel is not available back in the protected marina, but out on the river, just below the marina entrance. The park is for picnicking, but if you go to the trailer where the marina manager lives, telling him you are river trekking he will set you up in the front yard, show you to the hot showers, and may even offer to take you to town for re-supplying.

If you stay here at Dodge, wander down to the docks where the fuel is sold and chat with the "gathering of old men" which collects there each night. Ask for Bob Coleman and hear some of his river stories. For a good time buy Bob's book, "Grab a Bush" which is a collection of steamboat stories and yarns. Buy it in the fuel store.

SANDPIPER Marina 617.7 RIGHT
The entry is just past the "navy ships" on your right. Phone at the restaurant which is closed Mondays, open some evenings and all weekends like most marinas.

OMAHA CASINOS 614 LEFT
On your left see two large riverboat casinos where the meals are cheap (that is, if you only spend money on the meals). Phone and hotel rooms also. The city of Omaha is on your right, but is difficult to access. The best bet for access is supposedly at the park on the right, but it is hard to find from the river.

BELLVIEW 601
Watch for the bridge. Just below bridge is the landing area

PLATTSMOUTH MARINA 591.7 RIGHT
A nice marina with snacks and fuel -- if they are open, which they sometimes are.

PLATTSMOUTH 591 RIGHT
Landing at the ramp on right just before bridge.

NEBRASKA CITY 563 RIGHT
Watch for the bridge.

BROWNVILLE 535.2 RIGHT
Watch for the bridge and two "steamboats" on your right. One is in the river and is a tour boat, and the other on shore and serves as a museum. Take out is at the park and campground located at the boats.

Brownville is just a few hundred yards up the hill. This little town is a tourist town and deserves a visit, though it offers no fuel or groceries. There are antique stores, a health food store, ice cream store, a motorcycle bar but, best of all, Midge Mason's "Brownville House," the only place to eat in town.

Midge and her children run a first rate, homespun small town restaurant where the featured meal is a gigantic rib eye steak, which is good enough, but the walk up the hill is worth making just to eat some of Midge's home made bread. Their $2.00 breakfast includes an egg, gigantic hunks of Midge's home made bread, jams and jellies, and a gallon of fresh coffee.

Midge herself usually serves breakfast, and if you are the only customer at 6 AM, she is likely to bring her plate out and join you, telling stories of other canoe trekkers, and remembering her late husband who was a fishing guide on the Missouri River. Don't miss this stop. (and use their rest room which has really hot water for a quick wash up).

RULO 498 RIGHT
Tie up on right after the double bridge at "Camp Rulo River Club" which is neither a camp nor a club, but rather a waterfront restaurant open to

the public at lunch and dinner. The small J&B Grocery store is several blocks in town (population 200). Also, turn left on 1st. street to "Ye Ole Tyme Saloon" which serves meal and is located across from "Ye Ole' Washboard" (I am not making this up) a Laundromat.

ST. JOSEPH MO 449 LEFT
Like most large cities, St. Joseph is difficult to access. The best bet is to tie up at Riverfront Park, near the "Spirit of St. Joseph" riverboat. Exit the park to the left and head for the clearly marked Civic Center building then turn right when you see the Holiday Inn sign. One block southeast from the holiday inn is the Phillips 66 gas station and C-store.

In the 1840's and 1850's the hills around St. Joseph were packed with thousands of emigrants every spring who camped here waiting for the grass to green up west of here so they could continue on either the California or Oregon trail.

ATCHISON KANSAS, 423 RIGHT
A delightful mid-sized town renewed and restored after the flood of 1958. Tie up on right bank at "Independence Park" before both the low (RR) and high bridge -- watch for the picnic tables. Lunches and dinner available at the River House right at the park. Formerly the Kansas-Nebraska Hotel, it was restored by 15 partners, one of whom (Steve Busch) is now the manager.

Fuel is available at the Texaco station at the end of the "High Bridge" (up the railroad track or road). Get groceries at the IGA four blocks in town on Commercial street (the same street as the River House).

Here in Atchison in 1860 the famous "Atchison, Topeka and the Santa Fe" railroad was formed. Also, the never-found aviatrix, Amelia Earhart was born (223 N. Terrace Street). Also on the river near Atchison is where the steamboat once piloted by Mark Twain sunk (though later recovered and continued in service.)

If you decide it is time for a hotel, the Comfort Inn is about a mile west on US 59 (the High Bridge route).

LEAVENWORTH KANSAS 397.5 RIGHT
The town hosts the famous federal prison. A singularly decrepit town with a public campsite at the "Riverfront Park." Just after the bridge on the right bank is a ramp. To get into town pass the coast guard building downstream, turn right 10 blocks for hamburgers and double that for fuel. Perhaps a better access is down town at the new riverside park, but you'll have to climb a four foot iron fence... and when you get to town it's sort of depressing anyway.

KANSAS CITY 365 RIGHT
The largest city you'll canoe through on the entire Missouri and, of course, difficult to access. You could get out at the new Riverfront Park on your right just after the "Square bridge"

but all you'd achieve is finding some grass to sit on. Or perhaps you might try tying up after the next bridge (a suspension bridge) and trying your luck at the buffet of the Flamingo Casino, though the food at this casino is not as cheap as usual casino food. Most canoeists simple try to get through Kansas City as fast as they can, which won't be as fast as you want to.

FT. OSAGE/SIBLEY 337.2 RIGHT

A ramp at 337.2 right leads to the old reconstructed Ft. Osage, which was soon established after Lewis and Clark suggested the site as an ideal one for a fort. The tiny hamlet of Sibley is just above the fort, but offers nothing more than honey for sale.

NAPOLEON 329 RIGHT

Land at the grain elevator, cross railroad tracks and take Ash Street directly up the hill 100 yards to a cool little general store, a Post Office, and a few antique shops. No fuel.

LEXINGTON 317 RIGHT

Large enough to have just about anything you need, and small enough to get around. Tie up near the wastewater treatment plant at mile 316.5 right. Take that road (10th. street) up the hill 500 Yards right into the center of town. Fuel another several blocks. Lexington is a delightful town and worth a stop.

WAVERLY 293.5 RIGHT
Tie up at the "Port of Waverly" on the right bank just before the iron bridge. Walk up the road leading to a town offering a Laundromat (boarded up), a drug store (boarded up) and several other very interesting stores (all boarded up). On the other hand, the post office, nursing home, and funeral home are all open for business, so waverlyites can at least get their mail, grow old, die and get buried. If you are still alive, and are not using Waverly as a mail drop, you could walk another good hop out the road coming off the bridge to find a general store and fuel.

MIAMI 262.5 RIGHT
The landing is on the right just before the bridge. But there is nothing to land for- the town is virtually empty.

GLASGOW 226.5 LEFT
A wonderful river town actually right on the river and not perched on a bluff as usual. Tie up near the Corps of Engineers Quonset hut on the left bank just before the CoOp grain elevator. Just a block behind the CoOp is a gas station and the post office. To your left are several restaurants, a drug store, and other assorted small town non-tourist shops including a Laundromat. Glasgow is a great stop.

BOONVILLE 197 RIGHT
Tie up is either under the bridge or beyond the bridge at the "Riverfront Park." A nice medium

sized town which has not been Wal-Martized, and continues to act like Wal-Mart hadn't moved in at the edge of town even though it has. Boonville is a full service town with anything you want, ands is a wonderful place to wander around as you smell the delicious fragrance of a local bread factory right on the main street.

MARION 158 RIGHT
A "campground" supposedly, but nothing very helpful in the "town" itself.

JEFFERSON CITY 144 RIGHT
The capitol of Missouri but a royal pain to access. Perhaps you will tie up near the capitol building and walk over the Rail Road tracks into town. Better yet, like most large towns, you'll probably simply pass it by.

HERMANN 98 RIGHT
If you are trekking the entire Missouri you will probably try to make it to Hermann for two reasons. First, it is a delightful little German river town directly on the right bank. Second, it is located at mile 98 -- and arriving here signals your breaking the final 100 miles of your trek -- the end of the Missouri is in reach.

Tie up is at the Riverfront park on your right just below the bridge where there is located a small bait shop and a boat ramp. (Ask where you should tie up for the night if you are staying -- remember this is a German town and things must be done properly, and always by asking.)

Just a block back from the river front are a dozen shops, a grocery store, and several superb eating establishments. If you've got 80 bucks) right facing the river (214 Wharf street) is a hundred year old B&B in which to celebrate your final days on the river. If your tastes are more inexpensive, (or you wouldn't like Mary's cat) try the 1950's motel a few blocks up the hill at the end of the bridge.

Hermann was settled by a society from Philadelphia for the purpose of preserving German culture and language. Many of the older residents still speak German at home and the town is neat, clean, and efficient, as you might expect.

NEW HAVEN 81.7 RIGHT
A town which tried hard to be Hermann but failed miserably. You can tie up at the 81.7 levee marker to see a ghost town. There is a post office and a pub which is open over lunch time on some days.

WASHINGTON 67.5 RIGHT
Another German settlement larger than Hermann but not quite as nice. Tie up at city park and find everything in this town. Even fuel is available about six blocks up Elm street.

MISSISSIPPI RIVER 0.0
The Mississippi, "the largest tributary of the Missouri" enters the river from the left. Directly across the Mississippi at the confluence

see the Lewis and Clark monument, a nice quiet place to end your journey just 15 miles above the arch and surrounded by trees and natural river setting. If you want a more public ending point, go on to the arch turn by turning right down the Mississippi passing through the "Chain of rocks" to the arch on your right.

6

After Your Trek

Congratulations!
You've accomplished a great trek. Whether you set out to do a 500 mile section of the river, or the entire length, you've finished it. Celebrate!

Postcards.
On completion you'll want to send a postcard or letter to all the people who helped you along the way. A simple postcard is enough, ideally mailed at St. Louis (or whatever town you end at), or if you mail from home do so in the next week. Be careful of thinking you'll write later -- most trekkers who delay this duty never accomplish it. Those who helped you, and any other trekkers you met, will be interested in how you made out. The "helpers" along the way often identify with your trek, letting you take the journey vicariously for them. It is important that they know how you fared. (And it is important to their helping other trekkers they might meet in the future.)

Photos.
You will want to collect and mark your photographs. Many trekkers now use disposable cameras and get them developed in a 1-hour shop along the way, so as to quickly

mark where the photo originated. If you delay this task until the end of the trek you may not be able to tell one lake from another. Besides, most all your pictures will look alike anyway -- water everywhere framed by more-distant-than-it-seemed shoreline (unless you hiked to the top of bluffs and took pictures down on the river -- the best shots).

Presentations.
If you intend to give talks on your adventure, and you took slides or can digitize your photos fine; it is another way of sharing your adventure. Posting your journal on the Internet can also help other future trekkers.

Guidebook additions and corrections.
If you have made notes for additions or corrections for this guidebook, contact the author at kdrury@indwes.edu so it may be included in future updates.

Settling back down.
Be prepared to go through a bit (sometimes a *lot*) of trauma when you return to "ordinary life" following a major trek. You may feel "cooped up" inside a house, and you'll keep opening up all the drapes and raising the blinds. Your thoughts will drift dreamily to that campsite down in the Gates of the Mountains in Montana... or that sunset on Lake Sharp in South Dakota. You'll think often of the people you met -- even if only for a few moments when they helped you -- and you'll wonder how they are, as if they were best friends of sorts, or war buddies, now returned from the front.

And, be prepared for a few weeks of outright laziness. It is not uncommon for trekkers to go home and sit in front of a TV for an entire week -- incredible as that seems. It is as if all their "time off" was saved up for the end. You might consider this when planning the schedule for a long trek.

But, most of all, be prepared for people to not understand at all what you did. They will ask inane questions or make dismissive remarks. Be ready for "regular people" to be more interested in how you went to the toilet, than in the incredible journey you took. Forgive them,;they know not what they ask.

Which will bring you to a likely continued contact with any other trekkers you met. They will understand. Trekkers on the Appalachian Trail often maintain contact with others for years, even decades, sharing their common experience by mail. The same is true for cross-country bicyclists. However, river trekking is still a young sport, so you may have a short list.

Which brings you to getting in touch with trekkers from other years. Use e-mail and contact with the author of this guide to connect with other Missouri River Trekkers While you may have never met personally, you will have many common friends: Toston Dam, Great Falls portage Hole-in-the-wall, Ft. Peck Lake, Sakakawea, where you were wind bound, the wildlife you saw and where, and more. Your common experiences, though of different years, will be a long term bond.

7

Tribute to a River

I went on this trek interested primarily in the Lewis and Clark exploration. I returned primarily interested in the Missouri River.

Ultimately any river trek -- especially so on a mighty river like the Missouri -- changes the subject to itself. The Missouri itself quickly becomes your dominant interest as one uncovers the layers of history the "archeologist's trench" reveals as you float down stream.

The Missouri is a mighty river, much more masculine than the Mississippi, running faster and far less tamed than it's sister. The old story of the Missouri riverboat pilot who had gone blind reflects the attitude. His cheerful response to losing his sight: "Well, I can always go pilot on the Mississippi."

Formerly a Northward flowing river, emptying into the Hudson Bay or Great Lakes basin, the last ice age dammed up its escape route and forced the river southward to join the Mississippi.

For years it was considered unnavigable. As Stanley Vestal puts it, "Too swift for oars, too deep for poles, too crooked for sails, too shallow for keels, and too bank-less for towing."

It possesses a voracious appetite, gobbling up boats (450 steamboats alone wrecked here) river banks, cornfields, mighty cottonwood trees, and ranch houses for afternoon snacks. Each year it gorges itself on ten thousand acres of farmland, a few miles of railroad, and a couple hundred houses. It will swallow you too, if you are not careful.

It is a totally unpredictable, untamed, wild river in spite of the efforts to tame it with channels, wing dikes and levees and dams.

Never content with its bed, the Missouri puts it channel down where ever it wants to. The riverboat captains used to say, "She switches beds faster than any harlot." Some "River fort" sites are now ten miles away from the modern channel.

The story told most on the river illustrating its wandering path is of the Keane Saloon on Cow Island, which was on the Kansas side of the channel and thus legal to sell booze. However, in 1881 the river switched channels and put Keane's saloon in dry Missouri and he was promptly arrested for selling liquor. The "main channel" was then the dividing line between the two states (this case went all the way to the supreme court which made a fascinating decision differentiating between abrupt changes of the river course and gradual changes).

And the Missouri is ruthless and unforgiving. Want a gentile tamed river to float? Try the Mississippi. Want a wild roller-coaster ride down a river jammed with snags, logs floating along like torpedoes, "Sawyers" hiding under the current which bob up only once every few minutes which will lift any boat above right out of the water and dump out the contents. Or volcanic "boils," whirlpools, back currents, and quicksand? Canoe the Missouri..

And all this just describes the river section. Where the Army Corps of Engineers has tried to tame the Missouri with dams, the River simply collects all the wind available on the prairie and serves up a regular diet of rollers and breakers high enough to make you reconsider the whole idea of canoeing this River's route.

Then there is the natural history, and the historical-sociological influence of the river. It is a dividing line almost everywhere it flows, dividing time zones, cultures, and ways of living. On the north-south section you will find on the east side farms and farmers, and on the west ranches and ranchers. The people call each other west river folk, and east river people. For years the Missouri is "where the West begins."

Almost every emigrant heading west on the Oregon or California trail started their trip off with a boat trip up the Missouri. And we all know of the Lewis and Clark journey establishing the limits of the "Louisiana purchase."

Four state capitals are located on its banks, and for almost a hundred years it was the primary highway of the biggest business in North America: the fur trade.

While it no longer is a primary highway to the west, having been trumped by the railroads, then interstate highways, and airline routes, it still is a primary flyway for waterfowl, especially the section from Sioux Falls down to Kansas City.

But, this wild river can also be gentle and sweet. Reflecting blue sky and green trees with a setting sun, it can lie there calm as glass. There are stretches with high cliffs squeeze the river into a narrow channel rushing through at a rapid speed where sheep gather on the cliffs to watch you pass. It is friendly to all kinds of four legged creatures, even though far less so than the virtual petting zoo Lewis and Clark found.

It gives and it takes away. Supplying the rich bottom land for bountiful crops one year, then chewing up the acres the next to spit it out of it's mouth at the Mississippi. Farmers on the Missouri never know if their crop will be corn or catfish.

It is a restless river. Always moving. Always busy. In a hurry to make some unspecified appointment with destiny down river somewhere.

And is this the Missouri is brother to the trekker. We too experience this inner restlessness. We too want to be on the move. To be on our way. Trekkers are rolling stones. They have come down with wanderlust. To head off to some destined point down the river or up the trail.

We trekkers salute the Missouri River -- kin of trekkers.

8

A Short Book List

Books to read before or during your trek.

This short book list is not an attempt to cover all of the relevant resources to make an educational or for-credit "Floating Classroom" trek on the Missouri, but represents the essential basic books which can form a floating library. I read these books as I went, keeping some the entire trip, and rotating others through the mail to my home as I finished them, or passed through the area. At least every canoeist should carry Lewis and Clark's Journals to read each day, but I recommend working through all of the following literature on your trek or before it.

PREPARATION READING

The following books really ought to be read before your trek rather than on the river. But if you don't get to it before leaving Three Forks, at least read them when you are storm bound. In a group the books can be divided up and shared with each other. They are presented here in order of preference -- most important to moderately important:

1. Undaunted Courage By Stephen Ambrose ISBN 0-684-82697-6   Touchstone Books. This popular work by a reputable scholar can't be left out. While it is an excellent read on your trek, it is an even better preparation.

2. Thomas Jefferson & the Stony Mountains... Exploring the West from Monticello. By Donald Jackson. Before your trek consider this work which is both good history and good writing. Although Jefferson never traveled further west than the Appalachians, he is the single person most responsible for the US's westward expansion. This book is not a biography of Jefferson, but tells the story of how he came to see the need for a sea-to-shining-sea nation and how he pursued that end. It is the story-behind-the-story of the Lewis and Clark expedition and thus better read before the trek. (and some would argue *before* reading *Undaunted Courage*, since in these pages you will capture the larger picture of exploration including the unique competitive role of Canadian Alexander Mackenzie, who preceded Lewis and Clark to the Pacific by a decade but could not convince England to develop his land passage.)

3. Sources of the River, by Jack Nisbet ISBN 1-57061-006-1 Sasquatch Books.
A fascinating book recreating the true story of David Thompson -- fur trader, trader, explorer, map maker. From 1784 to 1812 David Thompson explored western North America recording in careful field journals accounts of the natural history and indigenous cultures of the inland northwest. Thompson was the first person to chart the entire length of the Columbia river. While it does not directly relate to the Missouri it is fascinating trek reading either before the journey, or on it.

4. Montana's Missouri River By R.C. Gildart (Montana Geographic Series) Available from Montana Magazine Box 5630 Helena MT (Or from Amazon.com). A great over all collection of typical "Geographic style" pictures and writing covering all 700+ miles of Montana's river. An easy introduction to this section before you leave and a great book to leave at home for others to follow your journey in pictures as you canoe.

5. Traveling the Missouri By Peter Lourie ISBN 0-382-39308-2 Simon And Schuster. Actually a children's book, but telling the story of a journey up river in a power boat (switching to a canoe for some of the shallow river sections) from Omaha to Three Forks. The pictures are accurate and it is an excellent leave-behind book, and you'll especially enjoy the pictures after you've returned.

6. Lewis and Clark: A Journey of the Corps of Discovery The PBS Video set produced by Ken Burns collaborating with author David Duncan is presented on two tapes over four hours. If you have a group going, watch it twice before you leave. Also, consider purchasing the companion "coffee table book" for the picture if nothing else. (If you are taking the trek for study purposes consider Ken Burns' PBS documentary on Thomas Jefferson also.)

7. The Moulton Journals Published by The University of Nebraska Press, the eleven volume set of the Moulton journals is the most comprehensive edition of the journals, but you will have to turn loose of more than $600 to get them, and if you are not intending to really take the Lewis and Clark expedition seriously for the rest of your life, the price may be excessive.

ON-THE-TREK READING

1. The Journals of Lewis and Clark, Frank Bergon, ed. Penguin Books, ISBN 0-14-025217-7
A must-read for any Missouri River trek. Actual journals with original spelling with helpful (but not too many) annotations by the editor. Great to read each night before covering the same route the following day. (Also available in other editions with other editors)

2. Montana's Wild and Scenic Upper Missouri River By Glenn Monahan No ISBN. A must purchase for your trek through the White Cliffs. Available from Northern Rocky Mountain Books 315 West Fourth Street, Anaconda MT 59711 Here is a mile by mile guide to the Wild and Scenic river jammed with quotes from the primary sources including journals and steamboat logs. This book supplies detailed history of the Lewis and Clark era, the trader era, steamboat era, emigrant settlement, down to modern times and includes chapters on geology, and wildlife. It is such a thorough book that you'll want to slow down through the W&S river section just to read it. You can also buy it at the Lewis and Clark Interpretive Center in Great Falls. Get it one way or another then mail it home at Ft. Peck to read again when you finish the trek.

3. The Journals of Patrick Gass, Carol Lynn MacGregor ed. Mountain Press, Missoula, ISBN 0-87842-351-6
Gass was a sergeant on the Lewis and Clark expedition and one of the few members of the expedition to maintain a continuous journal. His writing is simple and direct and he constantly reveals his love for life and an optimism about the trek. It is a great companion piece to the Lewis and Clark (more official) record and gives the reader another point of view or a "second witness" on the day's activities.

OTHER BOOKS AND RESOURCES
While few canoe trekkers will purchase all of the following books, if you have special interests in one or more of the following areas, consider these:

Indians: *Lewis and Clark Among the Indians* James Ronda The authoritative book on the interchange of the Corps of Discovery and Native Americans.

Natural History: *Lewis and Clark: Pioneering Naturalists* Paul Russell Cutright. Narrow focus on the 177 new plants and 122 new animal species discovered by Lewis and Clark on their expedition.

North Dakota: *Lewis and Clark in North Dakota.* A full third of the expedition's over all time was spent in this single state. This is a comprehensive look at the time.

Medicine: *Only One Man Died: The medical Aspects of the Lewis and Clark Expedition.* Eldon G. Chunard, M.D.

Sacagawea: *The Making of Sacagawea* Donna Kessler. Sorting through the myths and facts of the Sacagawea legend. Or *Sacagawea* by Judith St. George a happily told tale including the later years stories and myths.

Mountain Men & Fur Traders:
Courageous Colter and Company By L.R. Colter-Frick ISBN 0-9655788-1-0 A delightfully presented "the rest of the story" of this amazing member of the Lewis and Clark band who turned around and went west after the big trek, eventually discovering what would become Yellowstone Park

French Fur Traders and Voyageurs By LeRoy R. Hafen Full coverage of the vast French trading dynasty in the nineteenth century.

Most of the above books are available at amazon.com and all of them can be purchased through the mail order catalog of the *North Dakota Lewis and Clark Bicentennial Foundation at P.O. Box 607 Washburn ND 58577* (If you canoe the entire river you will stop here to see their dugout canoe, too)

About the Author

Keith Drury was captivated by the outdoor trekking life as an eight year old lad when he received a set of Zane Grey novels as a gift from his aunt and devoured the entire set in three months, then began reading the set through a second time before moving on to James Fenimore Cooper and other adventure writers.

At twelve, hiking with his father on a trail in the Delaware Water Gap, he met his first backpacker. When asked "Where'd you start?" the middle aged man said, "Wind Gap" some 20 miles away. Impressed that there would be such a long trail, Keith whistled, "This trail goes all the way to Wind Gap?" The older man chuckled, then turned the boy's head westward and said, "See those white markings on the bark of the tree?" Shaking his head he heard the man say, "If you'd keep following them you'd wind up in Georgia." As his eyes widened with the notion of a path continuing for more than a thousand miles, the lanky older man then turned his head the other direction and said, "And that way would lead you all the way to Northern Maine, 2000 miles in all."

Walking back to the car from their day's outing the young lad said to his father,

"Someday I'm going to hike the whole thing." His father wisely replied, "You could son... you really could... if you set your mind to it, that is."

He realized his dream of finishing the Appalachian Trail, along with other dream treks including a Florida - to - Canada bicycle trek and a significant canoe trek from Indianapolis to Mississippi, but even always there was this junior high dream to trek the Missouri River. One day he hoped to travel its entire length.

Husband and the father of two sons, his time was limited for such extensive treks until the boys went away to college and were married, and his summers were free with a faculty position at Indiana Wesleyan University limited to the school year.

In 1999, that little boy wrapped up inside a body in its 50's realized his dream, and the result is a guidebook for others who will likely follow in his footsteps, especially in the first decade of the 2000's when many eyes turn toward the Lewis and Clark Bicentennial.

To contact the author:
Keith Drury
4201 South Washington Street
Marion, IN 46953

E-Mail: Kdrury@indwes.edu